# Advance Praise for *The Upstander*

"Max Glauben's story is a tale of courage, resilience, and defiance in the face of the worst kind of human cruelty. Jori Epstein's compelling, compassionate, and intimate portrait commands not only our attention, but also our respect for a man who never surrendered his soul nor forgot what it means to be human."

—**Glenn Frankel, Pulitzer Prize-Winning Former Jerusalem Bureau Chief, *The Washington Post***

"It's not often that you'll find a story so well-crafted as this that it captures the evil Max Glauben experienced in the Holocaust, while never losing sight of the goodness that animated his life well afterward. This is an important book that will ensure generations yet to be born will know—on a personal level—someone who survived history and spent a lifetime opening the hearts of others."

—**Brendan Miniter, Editorial Page Editor, *The Dallas Morning News***

"I was nervous about reading Max's memoir, because I was afraid it couldn't possibly convey the hope and resilience that 'our' Max inspires when he shares his testimony at the museum. As I cautiously started reading, I soon realized my fears were unfounded. Before I knew it, I had finished the book with tears in my eyes. They were tears of gratitude that Jori had so lovingly and accurately captured the essence of Max— his history, his complexity, the twinkle in his eye, and his singular devotion to making the world a better place."

—**Mary Pat Higgins, President and CEO, Dallas Holocaust and Human Rights Museum**

"This story reminds us that the arc of the moral universe does not bend toward justice on its own. It is pulled in that direction by resilient humans like Max Glauben. *The Upstander* is required reading for the brave souls who have enlisted in the war against hate."

**—Daron K. Roberts, Founding Director, University of Texas Center for Sports Leadership & Innovation**

"A famous Jewish proverb tells us, 'Acquire for yourself a teacher.' I can proudly say Max Glauben has been my teacher. Max has taught me so many lessons about life, but most of all, he has taught me how to move forward without vengeance, how to remember without hatred, and how to be an upstander without anger. Read his story and you too will acquire the most profound and meaningful teacher you could imagine."

**—Rabbi Meir Tannenbaum, Director of Jewish Enrichment, BBYO International**

"From the gates of Auschwitz to classrooms across Texas, Max Glauben has spent decades channeling the most excruciating memories of his past into messages of resilience, forgiveness, and hope. Through *The Upstander*, Jori Epstein ensures no details from Max's story are lost to the passage of time. Those of us whose lives have already been changed by Max are that much more fortunate now that Jori and Max's bond is culminating in this remarkable book."

**—Rachel Siegel, Reporter, *The Washington Post* and author of *Stories of Moral Courage in the Face of Evil***

# THE
# UPSTANDER

How Surviving the Holocaust Sparked
**Max Glauben's**
Mission to Dismantle Hate

# JORI EPSTEIN

Post Hill
PRESS

A POST HILL PRESS BOOK

ISBN: 978-1-64293-784-8
ISBN (eBook): 978-1-64293-785-5

The Upstander:
How Surviving the Holocaust Sparked Max Glauben's Mission to Dismantle Hate
© 2021 by Max Glauben
All Rights Reserved

Cover photo by Tony Corso Images

Post Hill Press, LLC
New York • Nashville
posthillpress.com

Published in the United States of America

*To Max's family—past, present and future—and the souls he lost in the Holocaust. May their memory be for a blessing.*

# Contents

## Transformation

# A Moral Titan

imple truths emerge from complex stories. Jori Epstein's *The Upstander: How Surviving the Holocaust Sparked Max Glauben's Mission to Dismantle Hate* is a powerful and poignant example of such simplicity within a complex narrative. Permit me to explain.

Holocaust survivors were a small minority of the victims—many more were murdered than survived. Max was the lone survivor of his immediate family. The question survivors faced, the question that Max asked himself and Jori learned to ask in Max's name, is: What do you do with the accident of your survival?

There is a powerful Biblical story that I never understood as a child but came to understand only after I was immersed in the study of the Holocaust. Lot—Abraham's nephew—his wife, and two daughters flee Sodom, which is reduced to ashes. Looking back, Lot's wife is paralyzed and turned into a pillar of salt. Lot and his daughters dare not look back but travel on, looking forward and conceiving two great nations.

What can we learn from this story of destruction, survival, and new birth?

If, in the aftermath of destruction, one looks back too soon, like Lot's wife, one can become paralyzed by grief. One must move forward with the difficult but all-important task of survival.

As you read Max's story, you will understand how he rebuilt his life after the Holocaust. He survived by his wit and imagination in postwar Germany and immigrated to the United States. Only later—much later—did he begin to look back.

Because they faced death, many survivors learned what is most important in life. Life itself, love, family, community, security, and what Holocaust survivor and Academy Award-winner Gerda Klein calls "a boring evening at home." For Jewish survivors, the survival of the Jewish people became paramount. Jewish history and, ultimately, Jewish memory are about life and not death, no matter how pervasive death may be.

For so long, Max was silent, hesitant to open the wounds and confront the pain until a new generation was ready to hear his story. Yet once he spoke, he became so much more than what he—and we—could have imagined.

For many survivors, including Max, bearing witness later in life confers a sense of meaning in light of the atrocities they suffered. Survivors tell the stories of what happened to them to keep a promise they made to those they left behind. More importantly, they hope—however slim that chance is—that their stories can transform the future.

In service of this, the Dallas community and the Dallas Holocaust and Human Rights Museum have given Max a platform to teach and to become a beacon of conscience. He is a voice for pluralism and tolerance, for decency and humanity in the Dallas region and beyond.

Who could have imagined that little Max could speak in a Texas A&M stadium, a field normally inhabited by giant Aggies and their massive opponents, delivering a counter-testimony to white supremacy? The five-foot-two Jew spoke as a moral titan.

Survivors were first told: Don't go back to the camps. America is about the future, not the past. Progress, not history, is our most important product. But once Max looked back, once he wrestled with the pain and the grief, with the darkness and the loss, he found that going to the forbidden place empowered him. He found his calling, the reason *why* he survived.

Max responded to survival in the most Biblical of ways possible: by remembering evil and suffering to deepen humanity's conscience, to enlarge memory and to broaden responsibility. This is precisely how the ancient Israelites responded to slavery and the Exodus. It is how survivors responded to the Holocaust.

Max has enlisted young students as his allies. He speaks to all who will listen—again and again. Max transformed victimization into witness, dehumanization into a plea to deepen our humanity.

Max has given us all an important legacy along with significant responsibilities. Jori and the students who Max reaches in his talks and on his tours are the last to live in the presence of survivors.

Just as Jori Epstein has done so graciously, so compellingly, so movingly in this book, we too can become witnesses to the witnesses.

Further, we can transform what we learn from Max to better the world and prevent genocide. We can alleviate suffering and help heal its victims.

Through close work with the Dallas Holocaust and Human Rights Museum to develop its new Permanent Exhibition, I have seen Max's impact, charisma, and charm. I have been with him on the March of the Living airplane as he began his journey back to Poland. Even though he was four score and ten, he was energetic and driven, a man on a mission to teach, motivate and share his experience with the wisdom that has come with age.

Survivors such as Max have responded to three commandments that emerged from the Holocaust.

**"Remember: Do Not Let the World Forget."** Max fulfills that commandment every day in so many different ways, and now through Jori, his readers are invited to join in that effort. Max has been exceedingly candid in trusting Jori with his memories.

The Hebrew poet Chaim Nachman Bialik described the second commandment thusly: **"And in their death, they commanded us to life."** "Live life for each of them!" says Max. Not any life, but a life of substance and significance, a life filled with concern for others and responsibility to our world. Max exemplifies fortitude and resilience, a man who has found his own unique way to contribute to our moral betterment. Emulate him. Become his partner in this endeavor.

**"Never Again!"** is the third commandment.

Sadly, we live in a word where genocide has recurred time and again. We live in a world where some regard hatred as a mark of authenticity, where racism and xenophobia surround us, and where antisemitism has taken on new forms. Max and his generation have not defeated this demon. They depend on you to continue the task that remains unfinished.

And if you become discouraged, remember a truth that Max has lived: sometimes we must yell at the world to change the world, and sometimes we must yell even louder to make sure that the world does not change us!

Michael Berenbaum
Project Director, U.S. Holocaust Memorial Museum 1988-1993
Director, Sigi Ziering Institute at American Jewish University

# PREFACE

# Who Is Max Glauben?

I t's just before noon on a September Sunday in North Texas. Close to
seventy people from all walks of life gather at the Dallas Holocaust
and Human Rights Museum, gingerly finding their seats before the
survivor speaker program begins. Most aren't sure what to expect from
the five foot two octogenarian standing before them in his red, white,
and blue checkered button-down shirt. But the 2016 audience is rapt.

Max Glauben begins his talk. His sparkling blue eyes widen, his spir-
ited gestures animate each carefully chosen word. Instantly, he puts his
audience at ease. Max's thick accent has been subtly molded to the inflec-
tions of American English that he has taught himself during the seventy
years he's spent working and raising a family in the United States. But
that's not where Max begins his story.

Max begins with his birth in Warsaw, Poland on January 14, 1928.
It's a birth date not listed on his Texas driver's license, in his death camp
papers, or in many of the other legal documents that offer glimpses,
however contrasting, into his life. It is a life that has been checkered
with death.

He continues, guiding the audience through his prewar life as the son and grandson of newspaper owners, as a student of Jewish culture, as a Polish youngster doing his best to live life in spite of the festering antisemitism ravaging communities surrounding his own. Max remembers vividly the deterioration of what had been a safe life for Jews in Poland. He still can't explain why that deterioration happened.

Why, all of a sudden, did Nazi leaders force Jewish families like the Glaubens into a ghetto confinement? Why were Isaak and Samuel Glauben's newspaper offices burned to the ground, their neighbors eventually deported to labor and death camps? Max was just fifteen when the Nazis murdered his mom, dad, and brother. He was seventeen when American soldiers liberated him from the Nazis' hellish hold.

So much hides behind Max's wrinkled smile, his sparkling blue eyes.

So much is hinted by the crudely needled "KL" etched permanently atop his right wrist.

So many memories.

Max seems to remember them all, even as time elapses: the storied path from slave labor to liberation, from immigration to American army service. He remembers settling in Dallas to become a businessman, family man, and active member of the Dallas Jewish community. He remembers when—after so many years of silence, so many years masking the past—he finally decided to shed light on the dark history he had lived, to become a mouthpiece for the many who were killed and couldn't tell their own stories.

So Max will tell you that the 1.5 million children, six million Jews, and millions of others who were murdered in the Holocaust weren't just a mass aggregate of victims. No, Max will say each was a lost soul—a scientist, a musician, the next Albert Einstein, the next Elvis Presley, the next discoverer of a drug like penicillin. They were mothers, fathers, brothers, sisters, sons, and daughters taken from this world before their natural time. Max will try to fill their void and ascribe meaning to their lives after their deaths.

On this day at the museum—like on so many days for the last two decades—Max will tell you about his life. He hopes he won't make you sad. He's careful to infuse humor and charm into stories of the horror he has lived through; after all, pain can't be duplicated, he'll tell you. He wants you to be an upstander, not be depressed. He wants you to bear witness, not lose faith in God or humanity.

He certainly hasn't.

So Max will tell you, and he will tell an auditorium of 900 people in McAllen, Texas, and he will tell thousands more at Texas A&M's football stadium. He will tell small groups of school children and a room full of survivors gathered together in Germany. He will tell high school groups that visit the concentration camps in Poland he was once shepherded between. He will tell you his life story, answer your questions, and be a face you can pair with an incomprehensible chapter of history so foreign to Americans living in peaceful times. He knows that reconciling these disparate chapters of his life can be confusing.

Max hopes you'll leave not scarred by the death he saw but inspired by the life he lives. Max might feel like your grandfather. He's okay with that. Husband, father, grandfather, and great-grandfather are among the many hats he wears. He doesn't take family for granted after losing so much of it so brutally. He relishes family gatherings with his three children, seven grandchildren, and the three great-grandchildren now carrying his legacy. He enters a room humming, smiling, his glistening eyes hinting at the wisdom he has gleaned but belying the darkness he has endured.

The darkness is there, though. Nightmares and physical pain still plague Max. So do nagging questions about what and who he might have become. All of this lingering pain motivates him to ensure that the horrors he survived don't happen again. He longs to educate people who can't imagine what he's seen.

At Texas A&M in December 2016, alt-right leader Richard Spencer was speaking across campus the same day, preaching ideas diametrically opposed to Max's. Weeks earlier, Max had already spoken to an audience of more than 600 in the same room Spencer now occupied. But Max returned to College Station to preach unity during Spencer's visit. Upon his arrival, he greeted his granddaughter Delaney, a Texas A&M student. Delaney beamed as her "Zayde" crossed Kyle Field before a packed stadium.

"It's a 'whoa' moment," she said. "Hopefully hearing my Zayde's story will help them see what hate has caused."

They will also see how the desire to combat hate has motivated this Holocaust survivor to persist in three countries, six languages, and culture after culture for more than ninety years.

As the number of Holocaust survivors dwindles, Max Glauben preaches tolerance and strength in the wake of persecution and division. Max's chief concern in telling his story is to deliver testimony without creating hate. He wants to spur listeners—to spur you—to be upstanders, not bystanders.

"If you have any hatred, bigotry, or antisemitism," he says, "I hope that after you read this book, you might change your mind."

This book is the story of Max Glauben, a resident of Dallas, Texas, and a survivor of the concentration camps Majdanek, Budzyn, Mielec, Wieliczka, Plaszow, and Flossenbürg. This story is the story of one man. And yet, it is the story of so many. Max hopes it will never again be the story of any.

# UPHEAVAL

# CHAPTER 1

# High Pain Tolerance

Even as a toddler, Max Glauben was different.

Max was taken to the hospital, as the story goes, to have his tonsils removed. The doctors didn't put him to sleep for the procedure.

"I was real, real little, and the instruments were hot," Max says. "They burned my throat, and they didn't give me a sedative."

Then, the surgeon carried his three-year-old patient out into a room full of doctors and nurses.

"There's a kid whose tonsils we took out, and he didn't even cry," the surgeon bragged.

Max shrugs at how his earliest memory could have been a scarring—physically and psychologically—experience.

"My pain tolerance has always been great," he says.

He would need that.

Max "Moniek" Glauben was born to Fela Hoffman and Isaak Glauben in Warsaw, Poland on January 14, 1928. He was born on a Saturday, the Jewish Sabbath, which spurred family lore about a Friday night trip to the hospital. Max remembers elder family members later trying to convince Fela that Max was born in February, not January.

He just laughed; why would they know better than the mother who birthed him?

No one yet knew how important Max's birth date would become during the war.

For the first ten years of his life, Max and his parents lived an unencumbered life in their small Warsaw apartment on Mila Street, number 38. Max's brother, Heniek, was born two years after him. Fela presided over the household, cooking every meal and parenting the two boys, who shared a bed. Isaak worked in the newspaper industry by day and as a book binder and de facto community accountant by night. He had always been "arithmetically inclined," says Max, who inherited that gene.

Max and Heniek attended the local *Tarbut*, or Jewish culture, school, on Geisha Street. Max remembers going back and forth between Geisha Street and Mila 38, taking the steps two at a time up to the fourth-floor apartment each day when he returned home. He would then go to the neighborhood bakery to pick up bread and to the Mila 38 *shtiebel* (small synagogue in the apartment) for afternoon and evening prayer services.

Max loved visiting his father and grandfather's newspaper offices on Leszno (pronounced *Lash-nah*) Street. The family newspaper business was multifaceted: Isaak ran the Yiddish-language Dos Judisze Togblat (Polish for "The Jewish Daily") that appealed to more secular, Zionistic Jews. Max's grandfather, Samuel—Isaak's father—kept up Dos Judisze Express (Polish for "The Jewish Express"), which featured more traditional, Orthodox perspectives. Each appeased a "clannish" group of Jews, Max says, updating readers about everything from politics to the weekly Torah portion.

Paper distribution spanned greater Poland, France, Belgium, and more. An archive copy lists "all other lands" as a delivery choice. The Yiddish-language papers remained indiscernible to the non-Yiddish-speaking Nazis on the cusp of their 1939 invasion of Poland. Thus, the newspapers became a vessel of warning in a 1930s era of what Max calls "hushness."

"The Jewish people were scared," Max says. "Don't say anything—someone might hear you and hurt you. What the papers tried to do was distribute the news to the public at large because families themselves were afraid to say anything for fear that if someone hears it, they'd harm them."

Max didn't care much for the papers' substance, their advocacy, or their interpretations on the weekly Torah portion. He didn't speak Yiddish anyway, so he couldn't read the articles emanating from his father's printing presses. But Max loved watching Isaak fire up the presses for each new issue. He was fascinated with how his dad would count the copies of each issue, wrap a bundle with wire, twist the wire tightly, and then break the wire piece by hand. As copies piled up for distributors to collect, press workers kept count with a bell loud enough "to wake someone up if they were asleep," Max says.

He observed quietly and taught himself to use some of the machines. Max paid close attention as workers maneuvered the Linotype machine, selecting letters with a band and lever, then filling each in with a bucket of lead. No one told Max where to find the letters or how to ensure they materialized on the paper. But after he watched a few rounds, Max began cranking out his own stamps with the cylinder-and-paper contraption. Sometimes, he pressed his Polish name "Moniek"; other times, his Hebrew moniker "Mendel." Each time, he prided himself on finding a solution and making "a finished product."

"I was a youngster that never asked questions," Max says. "Because when I looked at something, I could realize how two and two doesn't make five or three."

Max wishes he could've visited the offices more often. But with antisemitism already festering in prewar Europe, walking outside Jewish quarters to the office at Leszno 40 left Max vulnerable to scrutiny from the greater Polish society. Polish children would throw objects at him. At least when the Jewish children were bigger, the Polish children sometimes retreated in fear, Max says. His parents wouldn't address the antisemitism explicitly. Max says they didn't need to. Any time he ventured outside his Jewish school, Jewish apartment complex, or the Jewish shops, he sensed a change in the demeanor of those around him. Neighborhood kids would taunt Max. Trips to his father's office on Leszno stood out.

"When we went there, if we were not hurt physically, we were hurt visually, and then maybe just verbally," Max says. "It was an environment I don't wish for anyone to live under. If you were not bullied and not hurt, the looks were killing."

He began to learn more.

The boxing gloves taught him one lesson.

Max was seven or eight, he estimates, and attending school on Geisha Street. The separate Jewish *Atid* school served two purposes. First, it enabled kids to receive a proper religious education. Max studied secular subjects like Latin literature, arithmetic, and geography. He also mastered the Hebrew language and biblical studies, in preparation for what his parents envisioned as their children's eventual immigration to the state of Israel, which at the time was still the British-mandated land of Palestine. Children didn't learn the Yiddish their parents spoke, but they learned Polish perfectly.

Jewish schools didn't provide only a home for religious education; they also provided a means of safety. Max says that kids learned to "be quiet—don't say anything—because someone might not like what you say and do something to you." Separating Jewish schoolchildren from Polish society helped ensure that feisty youngsters like Max didn't mouth off and get hurt picking a fight. *Atid* schools shielded Max and his peers from some of the rock throwing, name calling, and hat snatching. But the kids weren't completely immune.

At his school, Max says, the bully complex would carry over from the streets. Jewish kids who were victims of antisemitic bullying channeled their anger by bullying Jewish peers. Max remembers when a classmate tripped him on his way to the blackboard. They were probably eight years old.

Max's favorite teacher, Baruch, then told the students that this was not how you treat people. Baruch told Max and his antagonist, "You two need to settle this yourselves." Baruch then handed the eight-year-olds boxing gloves and told them to settle the spat in the gymnasium ring.

"I didn't knock him out, but I hurt him," Max says of the boxing match, which he never told his parents about. "I was real mad he did it. He was a bully."

Max guesses his athletic build ultimately gave him the winning edge. The boy never bothered him again. In fact, Max says, the two boys played as friends afterward. Baruch had taught them a lesson.

"Just like, settle your problems by yourself," Max says. "They taught us to take responsibility for your action. I think it was a good lesson drilled."

It was one of many nonacademic lessons from school that would help save Max's life during the war. The chief example was carpentry.

Woodworking class was intended simply as an extracurricular activity at *Tarbut* school. Teachers interspersed crafts and gymnasium weightlifting with writing and arithmetic. Remnants from nearby carpentry shops were recycled as materials for students' next creations. They made toy boxes, puzzles, and baby pull toys with wheels. Max took pride in always receiving a "5," which was the top grade awarded for projects. Max even pursued carpentry beyond school hours.

"We were playing sometimes, maybe kicking a ball," he says. "But I was more industrious or whatever. I played, but I didn't put too much emphasis on play. [I put] more curiosity in legs and how things worked— how the legs worked in things."

Max's curious explorations and early prowess in carpentry only dimly resembled the blueprints and airplane patterns that he would one day follow in concentration camps. His knack for symmetry and design would stick with him in those later years, but his creativity...not so much.

"If I needed a part for something, I could draw a square box and put down how many centimeters are there and all that," Max explains of his childhood designs. "If I wanted something to resemble something like a heart, then I could draw symmetrically."

In the concentration camp, this instinct remained, Max notes. "Because there, I didn't analyze anything. I just had to do it or I die."

# CHAPTER 2

# Mischievous Max

As a child, Max found time to enjoy family meals and to challenge neighborhood girls to hopscotch. He found time to cook potato pancakes and to adventure with Heniek. He also found time to get into trouble.

The reasons varied. One time, he was playing with a neighborhood girl when the two decided to "expose themselves" to one another.

"It was a natural kind of trouble," he laughs. "It was a sexual thing."

His mom was horrified and let him know it.

"It was probably kids' curiosity," Max protests.

Another time, Isaak took Max and Heniek on a Shabbat walk to see the new automat on upscale Marszalkowska Street. Max knew he shouldn't bring money along; handling and spending money is forbidden on the Sabbath. But he was curious how the vending machine worked. He put his coin in and accidentally selected the least kosher option: a ham sandwich. Strike two.

Isaak reminded Max that he had already violated the Sabbath by bringing along money. "Since you already committed a sin, eat it," Isaak said. "But don't tell your mom about it, or you'll be in trouble."

Max found trouble often. He remembers once stepping into a bucket his mother had positioned to drain noodles for dinner. "You knew the bucket was there," she told him as he cried from the hot water's sting. "Why'd you step into it?"

The "whys" continued every day, it seemed: Why did Max wreck an umbrella trinket on the shelf? Why did he stick the crystal from the radio antennae up his nose, wedging it hard enough to get stuck? Or was it a *grosh*—a Polish penny—that Max had stuck up there? He remembers finally blowing out whatever it was, then being unable to find it until Isaak discovered it had landed in his cuff. Each such incident brought laughs—sometimes only in retrospect. Other times, there was punishment: to your room, without dinner.

"Eventually they either brought [food] in or they gave up," Max says. "Because they were good parents. But very strict."

Max remembers this strictness from nightly family dinners and Shabbat. Family dinners were a Glauben staple. Isaak would return home from the office after another edition of *The Jewish Daily* had gone to press. Isaak would pour himself some schnapps then join Fela, Max, and Heniek at the kitchen table. A diverse food supply was still accessible to Jews before the war, so menus varied. Max savored the nights when Fela served gefilte fish, gizzards, chicken soup, rice, or beans. But, he liked chicken wings best.

Still, Max ate whatever was on the table, no complaints. He took only the portion he was able to eat, kept his nose down, and chatted minimally with the rest of the family during the meal.

"Some of us were really shy, even in the family," Max says, "because number one, [our] parents were real strict."

Max worried that if he talked too much, he would say the wrong thing or offend someone. He knew he would be chastised if he did. Warsaw in the 1930s bred a restrictive brand of parenting.

A "confined individuality," Max calls it. "We were told how to grow up, how to listen, how to walk, when to play, and what chores to do."

He admires that Western parenting evolved to encourage kids' self-expression and individuality. He also admits he felt clueless parenting forty years later in Dallas when he began to raise a family in a freer, less dangerous environment.

**Max (left) with mother Fela and brother Heniek circa 1937–38.** *Photo courtesy of the Dallas Holocaust and Human Rights Museum, Max Glauben Collection*

The restrictions of Max's childhood were partly cultural. Society wasn't as progressive as it would be in the years to come. But also, Jewish parents worried for their children's safety, aware of Warsaw's antisemitism long before it peaked in the atrocities of the Holocaust, before they would admit to their children what dangers lay in wait outside the neighborhood. Even letting kids play games in the park was a risk.

"We held back and weren't allowed to do all the things kids usually do," Max says. "The parents were caring about the kids, so they wouldn't let them go wild even in the park, because someone might harm or do something to them."

Food, family, and ritual brought joy. Max helped his mom soak and ferment cherries to make homemade wine for Passover. He cooked potato pancakes for Hanukkah, and he added the carrots and parsnips into the gefilte fish at just the right time. The whole family came together for the Sabbath, with Isaak always taking off work from sunset on Friday to nightfall on Saturday.

Max treasured his responsibilities in helping his mother make the Shabbat *cholent*, or stew. On Fridays, Max would help Fela load potatoes and vegetables into a ceramic clay pot. Then they'd pile in barley, kosher rib meat, and carrots. Finally, they added onion and garlic to perfect the flavor.

"I don't think I knew anything about celery," Max says, trying to recall the full recipe.

Then, Max and Fela would fill the pot with cinnamon, sugar, and rice so dessert could bake in the core as meat simmered around the edges—one of mom's many resourceful moves. Max would seal the pot, wrap it with five layers of newspaper, and use pliers to tighten wires atop the pot. The mechanism transformed the pot into a steam cooker.

Each week, Max would carry the pot to the neighborhood bakery, where the bakers were finishing their last batch of bread before the Sabbath. They'd number the pot, stick it in the large oven along with neighbors' similar dishes, and give Max a ticket as he prepaid in full before the Sabbath.

Around noon on Saturday, after prayer services, Max dutifully returned to the bakery to pick up the browned and delicious pot of meat stew. The Glaubens enjoyed the *cholent* for Sabbath lunch, they enjoyed the cinnamon-sugar rice for dessert, and they enjoyed the rituals—prayer services, candle lighting, festive meals—while they still could.

"I was free to do anything that I wanted," Max says of pre-ghetto life, "but there was always that little bitty knot in your stomach of fear that somebody was going to make some antisemitic gestures. I always had a chip on my shoulder."

⬤●⬤

Antisemitism in Poland and Germany heightened as the 1930s unfolded. The decade prior, Polish statesman Józef Piłsudski had extended Jewish civil rights as he sought to strengthen Poland against Russian—and thus Russian antisemitic—influence. But by 1930, the end of Piłsudski's second term as prime minister, his hold on antisemitism had loosened. Attacks on Jewish businesses became increasingly common. Restrictions on Jewish educational and property rights became increasingly stringent. Piłsudski died in May 1935. Germany instituted its harsh antisemitic Nuremberg decrees the same year.

Without Piłsudski, who had discouraged state-sponsored antisemitism, violent boycotts of Jewish businesses began to increase. Polish Jewish communities, including those in Warsaw, waited in fear of violent attacks known as *pogroms*.

Max couldn't understand why. What had changed?

"I think the ones who really suffered the worst were the children," Max says, "because a grown-up could understand better than a child why this happened.

"But for a child, it was very difficult."

Names of Nazi leaders began to swirl in his parents' conversations. There were business riots and strikes, days when "everybody was worried" and community leaders started pushing immigration to Palestine more urgently.

Max's uncle, Aharon Hoffman, seized that opportunity to leave Poland. When Warsaw's Jewish communal leaders arranged a marriage between Aharon and a woman named Tsipporah, Aharon left behind his Warsaw sweater-making business to immigrate to Palestine. Aharon would come back to visit around 1938, Max says, wanting to bring Max to Palestine. Heniek was young, anemic, and weak. But Max was ten years old and had learned modern Hebrew in school for just such an opportunity. Max isn't sure why his parents ultimately decided to keep him in dangerous Warsaw.

"Things just didn't work out," Max says plainly. "[Aharon] might have come back…pretty close to some turmoil that was happening to the Jews in Germany."

Turmoil, it seemed, was always happening.

The Polish ruling party formally endorsed antisemitism in its official platform in 1938. The Kristallnacht, or "Night of Broken Glass," pogroms raged the night of November 9. Rioters destroyed one thousand synagogues in Germany, which by then included Austria. They shattered windows of 7,500 Jewish businesses and raped and attacked Jews mercilessly. More than thirty thousand Jewish men were arrested and taken to concentration camps soon afterward. Hundreds died from the inhuman conditions. Others were granted release and began plans for emigration.

What did Max know of Kristallnacht as it was happening?

"The news wasn't out that fast," he says.

Max heard murmurs about synagogue and book-burnings, and that Nazi guards were looting and restricting entry to Jewish establishments, but his family had no radio to broadcast the news. Later, following other incidents, Max relied on hearsay and belated newspaper reports to string together accurate depictions of what had become constant attacks. Max found it was even more dangerous to roam the city, unsure which parts had been vandalized, and in some cases, destroyed. He did know that the Nazis' anti-Jewish laws in Germany were why Jews began fleeing from Germany to Poland. The Warsaw Jewish community, he says, wasn't welcoming.

"The problem was that the German Jews were Germans first—then they were Jews," Max says. "They were sympathetic with the German regime, so they were not too well accepted by the Poles."

Besides, the Warsaw Jewish community was struggling to look out for itself as Polish schools began banning Jewish students. Should families escape Poland while they could? Max's Uncle Shlayin thought so; but Uncle Shlayin's wife, Irene, Isaak's sister, didn't want to leave her hat business. So Shlayin left Irene behind when he joined a mission sneaking Jews into Russia. Ironically, Jews were safer in Soviet-held territories where antisemitism was formally outlawed than in German-held territories where it was the policy of the state. Max figured Irene was "stable and desired by many men," so it made sense she'd stay with the family. Still, Jews' economic rights were dwindling, just like their educational ones. Attacks against Jews became so common, they lost both their shock value and ability to galvanize foreign Jewish communities.

"You're looking out for yourself and your life and your food," Max says. "With all the things that are mixed in, it's just another historical happening."

He imagines his community reacted to news of pre-war pillaging the way much of Europe and the United States would soon filter out news of the Holocaust.

"We were bystanders for Kristallnacht," Max says. "But we were not the people who could become upstanders. Because we didn't have the power or the right to do the right thing."

And anyway, Max wondered, what was the right thing to do? Looking around, it seemed that the moral system he had been raised with was now turned on its head. He'd learned growing up, that if he did good, he'd be okay; if he did bad, he'd be punished. That moral simplicity had now lost its truth.

"My privileges were being taken away [as] punishment by these individuals for something that I didn't do," he says.

Max's number one question: "Why me? Why this change without an external change? I went outside, the same sun was shining, the same pigeons and birds were flying…. Everything was the same, but yet, due to the influx of a strange army, strange people, they took all my rights away from me. My misery had started."

# CAPTIVITY

# CHAPTER 3

# "Why me?"

The Glaubens took their last vacation in 1939. Like most families that Max knew, they would leave Warsaw each summer for a villa. Fela, Max, and Heniek left Warsaw when the school year ended, either loading a horse and buggy from Mila 38 or boarding trains on railroads that lined resort towns. Destinations included Polish cities along railroad lines like Katowice, 290 kilometers (180 miles) southwest, and Radom, 105 kilometers (sixty-five miles) southeast. Sometimes, the Glaubens rented more than one summer house in the same year.

The villas were inland, but even with no beach or water, Max and Heniek delighted in befriending young girls of neighboring families. They played soccer, hide-and-seek among the trees, and a six-sided wooden board game. Max would hit an inch-and-a-half sharpened wooden square with a wooden cleaver to see which of six sides the square piece landed on. When Max and Heniek tired from the sunny days, they took turns napping under an alcove of their summer home. The beams of the home lifted just enough for either boy to fit into the shady, breezy crevice.

Sometimes, Max would join his mom shopping at the village store. But often, they gathered supplies for meals from kosher vendors hawking products through town. They enjoyed *Smetana* heavy sour cream from a salesman who came by with a cart; Max watched as another vendor milked goats for the Glaubens. "Very, very, very fresh," he says. Without refrigeration, all products needed to be.

Most summers, Isaak arrived each Friday by railway to spend Shabbat with the family before returning to work. During the summer of 1939, Max expected that they'd retrieve Isaak from the train on weekends, as usual.

Instead, Isaak pulled up in a late-model Chevrolet limousine. With such unrest, Isaak explained, he needed to be sure he could return to the city at a moment's notice. When an emergency broke out, Isaak did. Max never knew what demanded his father's hasty return that weekend. Max believes his father's job granted Isaak more knowledge of the dangers facing the Jews than most had.

"He knew many things and sometimes he didn't want anybody to know," Max says. "But there were a few things that sometimes I overheard."

By September, Max no longer relied only on eavesdropping for the latest news updates. The radio blasted the headline as he returned home from school on September 1, 1939: Germany had invaded Poland.

The Glaubens couldn't hear every bombing from Mila 38, but members of the Jewish community warned them to patch each apartment window with masking tape in the shape of an "X" to stabilize the glass. They camouflaged windows too, a handy trick to shelter apartment life from the unstable outside world. And they stored sand on the roof in case faulty firebombs that hadn't detonated landed there.

"To make sure there's nothing that could explode after the attack that did not explode [during]," Max says, remembering the time he was among a group on the roof that found an unexploded bomb in the white sand.

They thumbed the firebomb curiously. Max estimates it was twelve to fourteen inches long and thrown by hand. A metal plate on the bomb bore indented letters indicating the bomb was manufactured in Spain in 1933. Max wondered whether the Nazis were already planning for the war six years earlier.

Max and his friends couldn't travel far for fear of the next attack. Their parents warned them not to roam. But he trekked up to the roof repeatedly until Warsaw surrendered on September 27. By that time, the Nazis had razed 85 percent of the city, which was 30 percent Jewish.

By October, the Nazis had established a *Judenrat* Jewish council in Poland to carry out their orders. By November, those orders ranged from confiscating Jews' radios and banning their train travel, to requiring that Jews wear Star of David armbands and clearly demarcate their Jewish shops. Suddenly, Jews couldn't live, work, or shop where they wanted.

"If you had any property, it was not yours," Max says. "If you were a professional person—a doctor, a lawyer, a scientist, a teacher—you could not practice your profession to the public at large. If you were a student and wanted a higher education, it was a no-no."

If the Nazis found a radio, they would kill the Jew who owned it. They confiscated the bicycles they wanted, too, though Max kept his and would later convert it into a rickshaw for ghetto transportation. And when the Nazis wanted to contain Jews in an enclosed area—what would become the infamous Warsaw Ghetto—Jews had little choice but to comply. They had to build the encampment themselves.

On October 12, 1940, it was Yom Kippur, the Jewish Day of Atonement. The Nazis demoralized the Jews of Warsaw observing the holy day, ordering them to build eleven-foot-high walls topped with barbed wire. More than four hundred thousand Jews were to cram into this 1.3-square-mile area, even if it meant crowding more than seven people to a room, packed in unsanitary conditions that would rapidly breed disease and hunger. Access to apartments, factories, shopping, and more became hyper-concentrated. They "had us fence ourselves in," as

Max describes it. The Glaubens already lived in the ghetto area, so they didn't have to move, but extended family and even strangers moved into Mila 38 with them.

At age twelve, Max didn't understand the implications of what his community was constructing or for whom. He wasn't on the permanent ghetto-building team, though he sometimes helped mix sand and water for mortar. At other times, Max would shuttle bricks to fellow Jewish masons. The construction wasn't fun, even for a young boy who had long loved carpentry.

"Not when you're hungry," Max says.

—•••—

Starvation was only one of many alarming health concerns in the ghetto, he'd learn. Accessible drinking water was also scarce, limited to hoarded rainwater or a stash from the Visla River when the Nazis permitted a trip there. Max accepted that hygiene was a luxury of the past. Strangers spilled into close quarters and drank dirty water. The abysmal conditions bred typhoid and whooping cough and poxes in epidemic force. The Nazis quarantined the Warsaw Ghetto, forbidding anyone from going in or out of the already-enclosed area. They demanded the *Judenrat* appoint two thousand Jewish policemen, called *capos*, to patrol the streets—so no Nazi guard would have to enter the plague-stricken area and risk falling ill.

Max caught typhoid. Heniek did too. Fela put a hot towel to their chests, applied Campho-Phenique, and infused water and hot tea with crystal saccharine. With no access to a hospital or pharmacy, Fela even crafted a homemade cupping-like therapy that she called by its Yiddish name, *bunkes*. Max remembers his mom dipping a wire with cotton swabs into alcohol and into a flame, then throwing the flaming cotton into a glass jar and cupping his skin with it. He remembers the smell of the campho and the tingling feeling in his throat after Fela mixed it with hot water. He imagines she'd stocked up on the salve before the local store ran out. Fela knitted in the bedroom corner while her patients rested. Max survived typhoid, but he was aware that not everyone did.

Max remembers when the piles of bodies littering the streets began to mount. In 1941, one in ten Jews in the ghetto succumbed to the lethal conditions. By that August, starvation and disease were killing five thousand Warsaw Ghetto inhabitants a month. Some caught lethal smallpox or chicken pox; others froze to death, "a sweet way to go," Max says. And when the quarantine ended, Germans rode bicycles through the ghetto for daily afternoon raids, machine guns ready to claim new victims.

Max shares gruesome details sparingly. But he remembers a woman who was breastfeeding her baby during one roundup. An older soldier—Max imagined he was Wehrmacht, or regular German armed forces, rather than a Nazi—stood nearby. Then a "young, punky German with a pistol came by," Max says, "and told this guy, 'We don't need her—shoot her.'"

The older soldier resisted. He wasn't willing to kill the woman, he told the punk. Find someone else to do it, he said. The younger soldier then pulled the pistol trigger himself, killing both the mother and her baby.

"I just felt sorry for them," Max says, recalling how this woman and child became the latest bodies to decompose on the ghetto's streets. "But after a while, how many times can you feel sorry? It becomes a way of life."

# CHAPTER 4

# Smuggling 101

S tealing, looting, and bribery became ways of life too, after the Nazis sealed the ghetto from the rest of Warsaw on November 16, 1940. The Germans allotted rations of just 184 calories a day per person, an amount so insufficient that—coupled with the unsanitary, disease-breeding conditions—starvation and epidemics would claim eighty-three thousand lives from 1940 to mid-1942. Isaak's work for the Germans sometimes merited supplemental rations, but still there wasn't enough food.

"184 calories," Max says, still appalled eighty years later. "Do you think you could live on a bag of Sun Chips or potato chips or two apples a day? No."

So Max began to learn tricks he would need to survive.

He paid regular visits to the bakery a block over from Mila 38, climbing atop the wooden planks of a shed at the nearby coal and lumberyard. The shed gave Max just enough height to straddle the metal fence between Mila and Moranofska Streets then land at the bakery. Sometimes Max would steal bread; other times bakers gave him loaves for free. Sometimes the bread was well-baked; other times he brought home deformed loaves that didn't rise properly. Max would toss the loaf over the fence on his way back, careful no one was around to pilfer it. Once he jumped the fence, he would snatch up his bread and return home.

Another tactic: sneaking to the freight yards outside the ghetto. Fourteen-year-old Max would see the farmers behind the Jewish cemetery and the boxcars from which they'd unload bulk food products, as well as the distribution buildings in which workers would organize those products for eventual transport.

Underneath his outfit, Max would stash a flattened bag or half a pillowcase, as well as oilcan spouts that he could use to puncture the burlap sacks full of goods. Max had at least five different spouts with which he could adjust the incision size. For sacks carrying rice or beans, he made larger incisions than those he made on the bags of salt, sugar, and flour. Potatoes weren't bagged in the first place, so Max could snatch them without needing an incision. He concentrated on supplies like these that came in bulk, so laborers couldn't keep track each time some small amount went missing.

Max paid special attention to the coal yard next to the Glaubens' apartment. Often, a horseman would transport manufactured goods, such as stockings, scarves, and uniforms, out of the ghetto. Max learned how to board the horse wagon when the horseman retrieved their horse, Lalka, from the coal yard stable. Then Max would hunt down available potatoes at the freight yard outside the ghetto and ride the wagon home. He grated the potatoes and made them into pancakes for his family, all before his father got off work. Max smuggled what he could, his Aryan-like blue eyes and curly blond hair helping to disguise his Jewish roots. But when potatoes were too hard to come by, the Glaubens' meals were reduced to bread and tea.

Max emphasizes the role underground resistance members played in his smuggling.

**Max among child smugglers in a May 24, 1941 German military propaganda photo from the Warsaw Ghetto. Max, second from left in the second row, is wearing a dark hat and fur-collared jacket.** *Bundesarchiv, Bild 101I-134-0791-35 / Ludwig Knobloch*

"I need to say 'we,'" he says. "I wasn't able to, at the age of twelve, negotiate this [by myself]....It was a united way of doing smuggling. Because singularly, it was too dangerous."

Resistance members schooled Max on the keys to subterfuge: Plan your route well, navigating the puzzle of roofs, holes, basements, and tunnels to travel quietly. Unsnap your Jewish star armband. Find bribable guards. Take what you can without getting killed. Potatoes, bread, rice, and beans were among the most common commodities—easy to travel with and easy to feed a lot of mouths for the amount smuggled. Sometimes Max caught a lucky break.

"There were some Polish vendors who saw the misery and saw us kids, and they looked the other way," he says. "They wouldn't call the policemen that we stole it."

Max estimates that 80 percent of the vendors he encountered would protest if they caught Jewish children stealing. Money assuaged some. Other times, a child never returned. Max wondered if they were killed or botched their travel plans. Sometimes, the lenient guard who allowed a smuggler to leave the ghetto had switched posts before the smuggler returned. If the new guard wouldn't accept a bribe, a child smuggling could be out of luck. Max never considered trying to escape the difficult ghetto life while on a mission—that would have been the "cowardly way." And he didn't just want to sit around while friends risked their lives to feed him. Max wouldn't smuggle every day but "instinctively and whenever it needed to be done," he says.

The risk was high. Max remembers one trip smuggling food beneath a wagon the Germans had commissioned to transport coal into the ghetto. Ghetto inhabitants were still initially permitted coal, albeit in limited supply, to cook and heat. Max remembers coal blocks big and small in the transport.

Polish kids swarmed the wagon brandishing sticks and canes with nails at the end. They hacked at the coal with the nails, trying to chip pieces off to steal. Max says he lashed out with a whip in the troublemakers' direction to scare them away. When the wagon neared the ghetto gate, the horseman told Max to disembark.

"I was left outside," Max says, "and that's when I feared the kids would kill me."

A Jewish policeman guarding the ghetto entrance saved Max. The details of his rescue blur in his retelling.

"I was so famished and scared, I don't even remember," he says. "Things like that are forgotten very easily."

As ghetto inhabitants' health deteriorated and new stresses mounted daily, much of the minutiae of life blended together.

"Each day becomes worse and worse and worse," Max says. "Sometimes your mind will dismiss some of the real worst days."

But one of those worst days in the ghetto he remembers vividly.

———● ●●———

Max was carrying an enamel pot of hot soup from his apartment on Mila Street, past the Pawiac prison, a couple blocks down to the Geisha Street 5 apartment where his grandfather lived.

Fela's father, Nachman, always appreciated the visits and food. Nachman's wife had died in the rancid ghetto conditions. His daughter Selah—Max's aunt—had been taken by the Germans earlier that year. She never returned. Raped and killed, they heard. Nachman was aging, though Max never knew how old his grandfather was. Max carried the potato-based soup to Nachman carefully.

But when Max arrived at Nachman's apartment, the front door wouldn't budge. Strange, Max thought. He knew the door didn't lock. Max fetched a neighbor for help, and the two pushed the door together until it cracked open. They found Nachman's body hanging limply from a noose behind the doorframe. Max doesn't remember whether his grandfather had fixed a belt, rope, or cord to the door hook intended for jackets. "I was devastated anyways," he says, "and you don't look for the details." But he remembers seeing the tightened noose and Nachman's body sliding down into a slouched position, his feet extended as if he were seated. Max began to cry.

"I felt what a tremendous loss he had," Max says, "and evidently, he didn't have anything to live for."

Max dreaded delivering the news to Fela. He also wondered how morally wrong suicide—an act that Jewish tradition categorically forbids—actually was. In such dire circumstances, was living really better? He understood both arguments.

———◆●◆———

Compromising Jewish laws, Max quickly realized, was necessary to survive. Max stole food for his family.

"Under those circumstances, I don't think that I ever felt like I was doing anything wrong," Max says. "I felt real proud, and I felt real good. It was a challenge that we were outsmarting the Germans…and the greatest good deed, according to the Jewish religion, is saving a life."

Laws of *kashrut*, or dietary restrictions, gave way too. With food so scarce, the once-strict Glaubens couldn't be choosy with their diet. No one hesitated when Max smuggled home a Danish ham.

"Well, we did well with kosher meat," Max remembers Fela telling their family. "Now we ain't got meat and we ain't going to die. As long as we have it here, we're going to eat it."

Isaak didn't object.

"When it's life or death, I'm sure God forgave many of us," Max says. "To this day, I don't keep kosher. If you're sincere in religion, your stomach doesn't know what you eat. It's your mind."

The Glaubens still said a prayer after each meal, big or small, rationed or smuggled, kosher or not.

"It was good," their blessing began. "It was excellent. If we had more, it would be better. But since we don't have any, we don't need it. *Baruch Chai Ha-Olamim*—Blessed be the One Who Lives Forever."

# CHAPTER 5

# Defense and Sabotage

Like so many, the Glaubens were assigned cramped living quarters with complete strangers. They lived in three different ghetto apartments over two and a half years. Bed assignments shuffled. Max and Heniek shared a cot at one point before ceding it to older relatives who had moved in with them. Privacy diminished. Max would cover his eyes each time his mom or an aunt changed into pajamas.

Sometimes strangers arrived at the Glaubens' home; other times, the Glaubens were sent to strangers. Max learned decades later that his dad would bribe guards for new jobs that offered a better chance at rations. With a shift in work assignments came a shift in apartments, the Nazis wanting laborers as close to their work stations as possible. Isaak dabbled in management, bookkeeping, and lumber supply after the Nazis burned the office of *Dos Judisze Togblat* to the ground in 1939. A Jewish news service, in Yiddish no less, was the last thing the Nazis wanted.

"The hate was so deep for anything that was Jewish," Max says.

The Nazis accelerated deportations to labor and death camps in 1942, expelling three-quarters of the four hundred thousand who had been forced into the Warsaw Ghetto. The *capos* reduced the number of ghetto gates from twenty to fifteen, further concentrating the population with regular evictions and redrawn borders. As the move toward liquidation left swaths of empty apartments, new opportunities for bartering materialized.

Max would join "hunting parties" to loot vacant apartments for gold, jewelry, and valuable relics. He could trade each such commodity for money, then use that money to buy food. On one such hunting expedition in 1943, Max remembers his party running into another troop.

"There was a standoff," Max says. "They told us to get out, and we said no, that we weren't going to get out. God willing, nobody got killed. But we eventually left because they got some reinforcements. We were on their turf."

The priority above all else in each risky mission was simple: survive.

"You are in fear," he says, "but—I'm going to get philosophical—we all possess a defense system. This is a part of our good brain that we have.

"This is the same way we live. You don't know what's going to be tomorrow. You're like an animal."

The Glaubens strove to be more than animals, infusing their restricted lifestyle with intellectual and Jewish enrichment. Max was still schooled, at least loosely, from 1940 to 1943, studying English grammar and arithmetic and Latin under cover. He remembers reading *Quo Vadis*, a Polish novel with a Latin title in the form of a question. The novel asks, "Quo vadis, Domine?" or "Where are you going, God?" It was a question Max couldn't answer.

He learned a Latin proverb that "times change and we change with the times." The phrase seemed to mock him. So did Cicero's Catiline Orations, speeches that questioned what civil liberties governments could grant safely. Max can still recite those Latin phrases he learned while paradoxically denied his own civil liberties. He chants syllable by syllable, his hands animated in gesture. A long memory was the goal: Memorize as much as you can, as quickly as you can. Read the lesson off the wall, recite it again before bed, and circle back a third time when you wake up.

Just as the Jews crammed into narrow ghetto quarters, Max's teachers were "cramming in as much knowledge and as much education as possibly was feasible," he says. Max joined twenty or so students learning hastily in whichever ghetto room was free and camouflage-friendly that day.

They carried on, amid apartment searches and shootings and regulations. They didn't consider it a choice.

"There is a certain amount of shock that can hit you," Max says, "and then it keeps on hitting and hitting and hitting, and there's a saturation point."

———•●•———

Sometimes, like when hunting for valuables, the ghetto Jews would turn against one another. If food rations could only feed his family, Max wouldn't tell his friends about a good meal. He guarded his smuggling secrets carefully, hesitating to tell even Heniek his tricks. Max feared someone would find out and encroach on his market. His rule of thumb: Protect yourself and your relatives first, even as the ghetto confines continued to shrink, and new families became your neighbors.

Other times, Max remembers partnering with the rest of his apartment complex to guard against German raids.

Kids and adults traded shifts. Max would stand at attention with rifle and Luger pistol while on duty, tasked with ensuring that no strangers entered apartment premises. Like other teen guards, Max would whistle loudly when Germans approached for their next raid. In response, his accomplices would rush to the nearest of the building's three basements. They always hoped they'd make it to the basement's side entrance or the one next to the garbage house before the Nazis descended. No one sought the stench of the hiding spot beneath the toilets, Max says. Some fighters would stay above ground to meet the intruders.

What happened to those Nazis?

"Sometimes we would whistle and get the German to follow us into the apartment," Max says. "And then God knows what happened to him. We just went hiding, but there were some underground people who took care of that.

"This was the way of defense and sabotage."

There were close calls. Max remembers one moonlit night on guard when a silhouette approached on Moranofska Street. He had his Luger pistol ready. The perceived intruder turned out to be Isaak. They went inside—crisis averted. The more raids in a period, the more Max would stand guard and sleep in the basements. They'd take turns from day into night, learning and cooking and praying after hours while the Germans—Max hoped—slept.

They cooked on open flames outside at night. Risking chimney smoke might alert the Nazis to their activity. The cover of nighttime was prime time for the limited Judaism the ghetto captives continued to practice, observing expressly forbidden rituals, always at the risk of their lives. Max remembers undercover prayer services including the Jewish memorial recitation *Kaddish* and the *Kel Malei Rachamim* prayers they said for dying neighbors. He vaguely recollects commemorating his bar mitzvah with a smuggled Torah scroll on the Sabbath.

"I didn't know what the hell a bar mitzvah was," Max says, "but I remember in our dining room, it was Shabbas, they brought over a Torah and I said the blessings. It was in secrecy and in hiding."

The ceremony didn't resemble a modern-day bar mitzvah or the cantor-led prayer groups that had met regularly in Warsaw during pre-ghetto days. There wasn't much to celebrate in the circumstances. But the gesture was yet another example of the ghetto "defense and defiance" Max takes deep pride in.

"The Jewish culture was alive among the dead," Max says.

The Nazis worked to kill it. On July 31, 1941, Nazi leader Hermann Goering directed Schutzstaffel (the Nazi military branch known as "SS") General Reinhard Heydrich to arrange for a "complete solution to the Jewish question." The Nazis wanted to wipe out the Jewish population.

In Warsaw, during the summer of 1942, they progressed toward that goal. Military and police forces joined to spearhead a mass deportation from the Warsaw Ghetto to Treblinka killing center between July 23 and September 12. They began the large-scale raid on the Ninth of Av, considered the saddest day on the Jewish calendar. They sustained the operation until Yom Kippur, the Jewish Day of Atonement. In fifty-two days, authorities deported and effectively sentenced to death an astounding 265,000 individuals.

Max didn't know at the time exactly how many of his neighbors were taken. But "we knew they were picking up more people," he says, and he knew non-Jews were eager to turn in Jewish fugitives and claim the rewards. The Glaubens wondered if they were more likely to evade roundups by hiding in one shelter or hedging their bets as moving targets. Either way, they would steer clear of the streets in daylight.

"The moral of the story is find a hiding spot," Max says. "Find a place you can hide where you wouldn't be discovered.

"This is where the resistance comes."

# CHAPTER 6

# Shots Fired

**B**oom. Max heard the first shot fired.

It was the night before Passover—April 19, 1943. Max and Fela were *koshering* the utensils for the holiday, knife by knife and fork by fork. Max organized ladles across a narrow table and onto a rack. There was a knock on the door. Max remembers one, two, about five people coming in. Or was it eight, ten even?

One of them had a German helmet. The rest wore regular hats and T-shirts. They carried rifles, pistols, and hand grenades. Were the Germans finally invading?

"No, no," the intruders said. "Everybody stay still."

Fela began to cry. The intruders ordered women and children to the basements. The order was in Yiddish, which calmed the residents. Still, Max refused. He stayed.

Soon, he learned these intruders were not Germans on a murder rampage but rather Jewish Warsaw Ghetto fighters launching what would become the Warsaw Ghetto Uprising. They belonged to the Jewish Combat Organization also known by the Polish acronym ZOB, for *Zydowska Organizacja Bojowa*.

It made sense for the fighters to set up camp in his apartment, Max realized. The windows of his Moranofska 11 residence overlooked Mila and Moranofska streets. Moranofska Square, the fighting epicenter, stretched in between. Max tried to make himself useful by bringing water to the fighters at their fourth-floor posts as they shot at the Nazis with their smuggled weapons. Moranofska 11 became the hub for an underground fighting unit. A couple doors down—was it Moranofska 9? The underground fighters were so secretive Max can't say for sure—the ZOB set up a hub for strategy and leadership. Bullets flew intermittently.

Max remembers the darkness. Hours bled together. Soon, he heard another shot fired.

Molotov cocktails, artillery, tanks.

"You better get your tuchus out of here," a fighter told him. "Get down there. It's becoming dangerous."

This time, Max listened.

He slid on his stomach down the artillery-marred crumbling staircase, tucking himself away into the Moranofska 11 basement.

Then he waited. For nearly a month, Max, Heniek, Fela, and Isaak joined a mass of roughly fifty thousand Warsaw Jews crammed into hiding in camouflaged basements. Sometimes Max tried to make use of the time, learning lessons by memorization. He learned English, Hebrew, and Latin in the basement, always unsure how much longer he'd live. Jewish songs about *glick* (luck) still linger in his memories, the lyric "What is my end going to be?" the most poignant.

But Max's teachers in hiding didn't always feel up to instructing. They, too, were hungry from the limited provisions. Everyone was. Much of the hiding time, everyone simply sat or laid down, keeping quiet in the camouflaged room.

"You were sometimes just lying like a dummy," avoiding capture, Max says. "[We knew] we were all human beings that were fair game for the Germans. It's really hard even now to describe how the things were working."

At times, Max says, he did catch fresh air outside the basement. He remembers smuggling escapades during the uprising, though he's not sure whether some smuggling memories date back to before or during his time spent hiding in the basement. One thing Max knows for sure: he was an attractive smuggling choice to Jewish resistance leaders for several reasons.

To start, he drew less attention as a fifteen-year-old than grown adults, he says. His compact frame took up less space as he maneuvered into wagon cavities when he needed to hide. Max's blond curly hair and blue eyes passed easily for those of an Aryan. He didn't observe Jewish law too strictly for the gig.

"When you're religious," Max says, "there's certain things you will not do."

Max grew up in a kosher home and still followed many traditions. But he didn't have the *peyes*, or sideburn ringlets, that clearly revealed the religious identity of more observant ghetto children. He accepted missions on the Sabbath, an easier day for smuggling, as some Nazi guards took off work for the weekend.

Max also lived next to the lumberyard, from where many smuggling missions were launched. He could receive instructions without even needing to leave home.

But Max's convenient address, Aryan looks, and flexible observance paled in comparison to his favorite reason why he suspects the underground picked him to smuggle, the reason Max was most proud of then and is still proud of into his nineties.

"I was always a go-getter," Max says. "I was always organizing. So when I was hiding, I was doing something. Evidently somebody noticed this is a good kid that could do it and have enough guts to do it."

What, exactly, did he need guts to do? That was less clear to him. Even in the moment, Max rarely knew what mission he was on. Members of the Jewish underground shared as few details as possible to minimize how much information the Germans could pry from him.

"If they asked me who, what, where," Max says of Nazi guards, "I'd be a dead duck."

Sometimes resistance members gave Max envelopes; other times they sent him on transports for mysterious goods. One time, an underground member said the transport would be more dangerous than usual. Max didn't know specifics but wondered if it was his turn to bring gun powder into the ghetto. Max jokes that he was sometimes hired "like an Uber guy."

He smuggled mainly with his horse and wagon but occasionally was directed through the sewer systems. A leader would instruct him where to turn right or left in the grimy passageways. Some sewers had even been marked with directions. Max shuddered as resistance members hastily lifted a sewer lid and shoved him into its opening.

"They just put you in real fast," he says. "It was more than once but…it's hard to describe what it is. You really want to forget it because you get scared."

"It was very dangerous."

The sewers were also a mess. Max's already-worn out clothes became further marred by filthy sewer water and rips.

Max didn't like it at all.

So he focused more on missions above ground, often aboard coal transports in and out of the ghetto, in search of food to eat and fuel to cook, burn, and heat. He'd always look to maximize the missions, grabbing the odd potato or sugar cube he might find at a freight yard to stash in a wagon crevice for his family. He knew each such grab risked the success of his mission, but Max scoffed at the prospect of returning to his family empty-handed when he had the opportunity to bring something to them. He found the risks exhilarating, and a "do-good grin" would spread across his face each time he succeeded.

"I cheated," Max says. "I was a general flunky. Not a flunky in the good way. A flunky is somebody that never does the right thing.

"But I'm trying to tell you: I always looked out for my interests."

Back in the basement, the Glauben family would share in the scraps Max stole. They built fires from rubbish for cooking and gathered wood that they would burn for heat. Before the uprising, they had stripped the casing from electrical trolley wire and attached the copper inside to pipes and rocks, generating electric currents that would flash in the darkness. But during the uprising, it was harder to find such material. The stakes were higher. Any contraption for light was welcome. And so the Glaubens and their neighbors constructed carbide lamps to illuminate their hiding places.

As many as eighty to one hundred people would hide at one time in a basement shelter behind the ovens of the bakery on Mila Street. Its insulation provided some protection from artillery while also masking the screams of frightened Jews inside. But the room became oppressively hot as the Nazis increasingly resorted to setting fires inside the ghetto. The heat suffocated some who sought refuge in the room. Others died from dehydration. Max remembers a baby who died in its mother's arms. He didn't know whether the baby was a boy or girl or at what point the crying baby's quiet turned from calm to death. But he thinks the baby suffocated when the mother muffled its screams with a pillow—one of many costly sacrifices the basement dwellers made to avoid capture and death for them all.

News reached the basement infrequently during the uprising. Trips out were rare, although Max thinks he still risked jumping over the fence to smuggle from the bakery at least once during that period. He could often hear reverberations from gunfire.

As early as 1942, Max heard murmurs about death camps. The Nazis were trying to deport five thousand Jews a day from Warsaw to the death camps of Treblinka and Majdanek. They rounded up nearly three hundred thousand Warsaw Jews that summer. But the SS didn't always have enough manpower to guard the large trains used to transport the prisoners. Occasionally, a prisoner escaped from the trains, returning to Warsaw and reporting on the horrors of the gas chambers and crematoria, where Nazis murdered and incinerated victims' bodies. There were also occasional rumors of a camp escapee.

Even among long-suffering ghetto fugitives, reports of death camps were hard to fathom.

"It was so bad it wasn't believable," Max says. "We started realizing it was a mass-murder type of thing."

Max's parents rarely discussed the future. He didn't worry much about what seemed like their inevitable deportation. He operated only in the moment. That wasn't reassuring either, however, as their hunger took precedence. Though Max was scared, wondering which day the Nazis would come after his family, most days Max was too malnourished to consider a tomorrow.

"You don't know what the next day will bring," Max says. "You just live day to day to day, from day to day. You never think about a future, and you never know what you're going to do.

"You just become like an animal that lives in the wilderness."

While the Glaubens focused on the present, the *Zydowska Organizacja Bojowa* resistance leaders had spent more than eight months mobilizing for an uprising to better their future. The mass-extermination reports, the ghetto fighters decided, left them no choice. Twenty-three-year-old commander Mordecai Anielewicz organized their efforts.

First, ZOB fighters armed with pistols derailed a forced deportation in January 1943. The Nazis actually hadn't yet decreed the ghetto's liquidation, merely thinning out its number, yet the ZOB thought they did. But resisting any Nazi efforts was a win. ZOB fighters then turned their focus to large-scale resistance.

During the Warsaw Ghetto Uprising in April and May 1943, resistance members fought back with pistols, homemade grenades, and some automatic weapons. They drove the unexpecting German troops outside the ghetto walls in what became a twenty-seven-day stand as war continued to rage across Europe. Seven thousand Jewish ghetto residents were killed on the spot across the four weeks; another seven thousand were deported to a killing center in Treblinka. The Warsaw uprising was "a big thorn in [the Nazis'] side," Max relays proudly. It would inspire later uprisings at camps, including Treblinka. Max mostly stayed in hiding but remembers seeing the Germans try to penetrate the ghettos on his rare trips outside. He marveled as resistance members threw Molotov cocktails. Max still is unable to fathom what happened that month. How did he survive?

"You don't know all the things we did in order to survive," he says. "Somehow we spend the time doing it, and I don't know if after a while you could even register all the things that you did.

"I can close my eyes and see males and females jumping from balconies…."

On May 13, 1943, the uprising was over, although the ghetto would continue to burn for three more days, and many fugitives along with it. Max remembers intense heat, a "real bad" fire in his Moranofska Square basement shelter. Rubbish and bricks fell everywhere. SS guards with rifles and bayonets ordered the forty-two thousand survivors into the ghetto square. They found the Glaubens in a bunker and ordered Max and his family into the streets with their hands up while the flames kept raging. Fela hastily passed Max a clay pot full of *schmaltz* (chicken fat) to hide between his legs. He didn't know why. Then the Nazis began disrobing Jews and searching the crevices of their bodies. They never searched Max, but he cried when he saw his mom violated.

When they were back together without the SS present, Fela told Max to reach into the pot. Inside, he found a shoe-polish box, and buried deep within it, jewelry.

"Dispose of it," Fela said. "Because if they catch us, they are going to kill us."

Max dug a ditch and buried the jewelry—their last valuable barter.

Earlier, they had worn cloth money belts, but Max doesn't remember when they ditched them. Isaak had given Max and Heniek strips of a white sheet to hide beneath their clothes as their basement hideout disintegrated, and the entire ghetto along with it. Fela tied the belts onto her sons. Did Isaak snatch them back to protect his sons on their way out of the basement? Did Max still have the money—wrapped in a simple white sheet—when they made it to Moranofska Square? Minutiae like that escape Max's memory, but he knows that he and Heniek would have been killed on the spot had the SS found the belts on them.

All along, the officers were shooting Jews at Moranofska Square, the same place where ghetto fighters had begun their resistance efforts a month earlier. Now, the surviving thousands were shoved into boxcars in the freight railroad yard. Nazi soldiers used the butts of their rifles to hurry along anyone boarding too slowly. Max, Heniek, Fela, and Isaak all boarded the same car. Max's immediate impression was that it "wasn't a good-smelling boxcar"; the stench of decaying bodies, urine, and feces pervaded every inch.

Some passengers drank their own urine to stave off dehydration. Others reached for condensation bubbles with which to wet their lips. Many screamed and cried; some prayed the traditional biblical verses of the *Shema,* and others simply "went berserk," Max says.

The Nazis crammed the Warsaw Ghetto survivors in the boxcar as tightly as possible, unconcerned with who might survive the trip. Many didn't. Sitting and lying down were nearly impossible, and standing was painful. Max took a headcount during the journey, at one point counting around one hundred people in the car that was twenty-six feet long, nine feet wide. He hummed along with the rhythm of the boxcar wheels to keep his mind occupied. The cars rumbled through several Polish towns. Max wondered how he ended up here.

"We looked out the window, and the skies were blue, and there weren't too many clouds in the sky," he remembers. "These thoughts were going through us: 'Why? For not doing anything, why did it happen to us? Where are we going?' Everybody was asking, but I don't think anybody knew the answer."

Five days later—Max's estimation from counting the rising and setting sun—the train stopped. They had made it to Lublin, Poland, adjacent to the death camp of Majdanek. Max waited for something to happen.

Then the doors unlatched, and the shouting began.

"Fast!" guards yelled at the malnourished travelers, unloading them by force if they didn't obey. After days of being wedged awkwardly in a boxcar, some passengers found their legs were nearly broken; they fell right there and never even reached the death camp.

"Stay with me," Isaak told Max.

# CHAPTER 7

# Skirting Death

Shouts of "Women and children, file up!" filled the air. Jews lined the winding road, marching five-wide as requested, awaiting commands. "To the left," some heard, gas chambers and crematoria awaiting them.

"To the right," guards told others, including Max and Isaak. They were now designated laborers.

Heniek and Fela, like most women and children, were sent left. Max didn't know where they were going. He didn't have much energy to process the scene playing out at dusk. Were Fela and Heniek on their way to showers and new clothes before the Glaubens reunited? The Nazis permitted the family to stay together in the ghetto, so Max didn't yet assume he'd never again see his mother or brother. He didn't yet feel the pang of loss at their separation, the first time in his fifteen years of life that Max would leave his mother for any extended period of time. He didn't yet grieve for Fela, who would, days later, be thrown onto a truck with other prisoners who were too weak to work and thus, by Nazi standards, too weak to live. Max didn't yet wonder what would happen to Heniek next.

Instead, Max focused on clinging to his father. At fifteen, Max was as tall as Isaak. He hoped he could blend in with the older, relatively fit men selected to join the labor force. It worked. No Nazi protested as Max and Isaak joined a group of about one hundred men selected for labor. They had no idea where they were headed.

Officers ordered the group to sit cross-legged in the grass and wait. Selections swirled around them, with trainloads of more passengers arriving, bringing more work-or-death rulings. Night began to fall. Max noticed the lights of the city of Lublin shining in the distance, unconcerned. In the dark, Max's group was moved to a temporary labor barrack. The hard metal floors of the portable building felt cold even in May. They spent the night there, receiving just a single meal of soup and a piece of bread before their next transport. Within a day or two—the details blur through hunger and cold, Max says—they arrived at Lager Budzyn, a labor camp beside a German airplane factory, forty-three kilometers west of Majdanek.

A surviving document records their arrival at the military-industrial complex on May 28, 1943.

A single-wire fence greeted inmates in front of Budzyn. A double wire electric fence guarded the rear of the camp, near the outhouse. There was no plumbing where Max would sleep. Max felt like an animal as the Nazis rushed his unit along through the camp.

The Nazis told new arrivals they'd need to shower and shave. Max worried: Was this a real shower or the deceptive gas chambers that he had heard rumors about in the portable holding building in Majdanek?

He breathed a sigh of relief when he saw soapy water outside the alleged shower barrack. Maybe this was just a shower.

Max's group was led into a first room, where they were instructed to undress and throw their clothes in the corner. In the next room, barbers buzzed their hair short—maybe to half an inch, Max estimates. Then came the showers: six to seven people per faucet, cold water, and brown soap with lye that left skin and eyes red. One minute in the water, an interval with soap, then one more minute in the water. A powerful firehose spray washed off the entire group at the end. They clung together in hopes of withstanding the force, but their combined strength wasn't enough. Everyone in the group was knocked to the ground.

"It becomes a mound of human beings…the pressure, if you're on top, kills you," Max says. "It did some people. And you get squashed if you're on the bottom."

Next came DDT as disinfectant. In retrospect, it made sense that the Nazis would use a pesticide on prisoners they considered subhuman. Max watched as they distributed "new" clothes that clung to wet bodies. The showers, like so much of the camp experience, were part of the deceit: this time for cleaning, but other times for exterminating. A "cowardly" way to kill, Max thought.

The process would repeat every few weeks. Max and the other prisoners received pants, a jacket, and a shirt that often didn't fit their new owner. Lucky prisoners traded among themselves to snag a better fit. Shoes were sometimes no more than wooden slabs. Underwear and socks were privileges not granted.

The prisoners lived in barracks resembling square barns, with beds stacked three or four high. The hay in their lumber bred lice. Winters brought cold so brutal, that Max remembers two of his toes turning black from frostbite. Summers meant stifling, claustrophobic heat. The prisoners—Max estimates three hundred to four hundred in a barrack—weren't given blankets or pillows. Max would lay his head on his right arm each night in place of a pillow. Even after the war, he would never stop sleeping with his head on his arm.

He dreamt often in the camps, the most vivid a recurring nightmare that he was being chased but couldn't run. He still has that dream more than three-quarters of a century later. But in the camps, nightmares weren't confined to bedtime.

"I would say they were dreams that were bad," Max says, "but what you got up to was worse. It was like a continuation of misery."

Isaak and Max were assigned to dig ditches at Budzyn. As prisoners, they were sent on regular marches. One Friday within weeks of Max's arrival, laborers were marching back to their barracks. They stopped at the outhouses on the way. When they returned, officers claimed three inmates were missing. Max reckons the inmates in question were left behind in the outhouses because the guards were impatient and insisted on moving along quickly. Even so, commanders took ten "hostages" per missing inmate and threatened to kill them if the escapees didn't come back. Isaak was among the ten. Max begged guards to take him, too.

"I'm going with him," Max told the SS guard who took his father.

The guard refused, Max says, and the fifteen-year-old protested—usually an offense punishable with immediate execution. Max figures the guard decided he'd rather make Max suffer through camp life without his father than let him die on his own terms. The guard shoved Max back into the barrack without Isaak.

Isaak's final message to Max: "Control your temper, and you'll survive."

The next morning, Max found a jumble of shoes and beaten hostages, lined neatly in a U-shape ten by ten by ten in the Budzyn *appel,* or town square.

The mangled bodies, Max learned, belonged to the only survivors. Max thought he recognized one man's face from Warsaw. Stray shoes, among which Max recognized Isaak's army boots, indicated remains of those who had been murdered.

Max says he didn't look any further once he saw those boots. He immediately understood that at age fifteen, just three weeks after his imprisonment at the labor camp, he was now an orphan.

Isaak's exact date of death is unclear. That week, Max remembers fellow prisoners marking the new Jewish month of Sivan, which would have fallen on Friday, June 4. Another post-liberation document records Isaak's death as early as May 28, corresponding to the 23rd day of the Jewish month of Iyyar. Based on that document, Max commemorates the deaths of Isaak, Fela, and Heniek together each year on the 23rd of Iyyar.

Whether he was orphaned on May 28 or June 4, Max remembers feeling insecure and "scared to death" at the sight of Isaak's now-owner-less boots. But soon after, Max's fear morphed into anger and defiance. He realized the Glauben namesake now lay with him and him alone.

"I must, even as a young kid, continue my name," Max thought.

His fist clenches, and his voice turns to a growl, as he recalls the moment: "I don't want—could not—give them the satisfaction of killing me.

"I'd do anything to outsmart them."

———◆•◆———

Outsmarting the Nazis wouldn't prove easy. Max witnessed cruelty every day. He remembers assemblies at the same camp square where he found his dad's shoes. Budzyn's commander, SS-Oberscharfuhrer Reinhold Feiks, would ride in on his white horse and demand a gathering regardless of the weather. A Nazi soldier in charge of the barracks would deliver a report. Then the thirty-four-year-old Feiks would cross the lines of prisoners, a pistol ready in one hand, a whip in the other. Sometimes he whipped Jewish prisoners so hard they fell to the ground. Max remembers times Feiks falsely accused prisoners of crimes like theft before exacting punishment. The commander didn't look his victims in the eye. He trotted behind the group to select which Jews to beat.

"Hanging and shooting is too good for the Jews," Max would think with bitter irony.

Feiks doled out torture directly and by proxy. Sometimes, he'd ride his motorcycle, trampling prisoners and maiming them. Other times, Feiks would mount his white horse, gather the reins, wrap them around a prisoner's neck, and whip the prisoner. He'd then drag the man by the reins down the line of prisoners, commanding every prisoner to beat his fellow inmate.

"By the time he was half-finished," Max says, "the guy was—I couldn't say black and blue then, but he just fell down, so he pulled him."

Officers would set the man down, propping his body against the building. Was he alive? The Germans took out a cigarette lighter, burning the prisoner's nose to find out.

"Brutality that was happening," Max says.

None of this quenched Max's will to live or his faith in God. Survival became a matter of defiance, like a kid who wants a toy, Max says, and tells his parents he'll do anything to get the coveted possession. Life beyond the camps was Max's coveted nonpossession.

"I didn't want to give them the satisfaction that they're going to kill me," he says. "There's a pride in proving somebody wrong and the mere fact that they *said* they were going to kill all the Jews—I said, 'I hope I'm not one of them.'"

Max prayed to God regularly, never losing his belief or hope that he'd make it, he says. He avoided confrontation or attention, knowing the more the Nazis recognized him, the more likely he'd become the next victim of their brutality.

"Quiet and shy," Max describes his camp persona, "and…just taking whatever comes my way."

He'd growl internally rather than complain aloud.

That is, until the day Max found an opportunity to speak up. After that, he didn't dig ditches in Budzyn much longer.

# CHAPTER 8

# Sweep No More

## Budzyn, Poland—1943

Max says officers often asked for inmates with specialized talents. "Does anyone have electrician experience?" they asked one day. "How about plumbing? Carpentry?"

A carpentry gig meant indoor labor, which meant better protection from the elements. Most prisoners wore just a shirt, a pair of pants, and maybe—if you were lucky—a jacket.

Max had been mechanically inclined for years. He thought back to the top grades he had received on his woodworking assignments in school, and so he volunteered for carpentry. The Nazis transferred him from digging ditches to an inside shop. At fifteen, he wasn't immediately assigned to build anything, just sweep the floors, apron on, per an officer's instructions. But Max's hyperactive mind craved a more productive assignment.

"The work made me too lazy," Max says. "Doing something that doesn't mean anything…was bothering me, when I knew that even for the wrong case, I could be useful."

One day, Max watched as the foreman of the carpentry shop, a man named Keller, glued together some boards. Max knew Keller was a German officer. He never learned whether Keller's official position was in the Nazi party or as an officer for Wehrmacht, the German military. What Max could discern was that Keller—whose first name he never learned—was struggling to glue boards together as straight as they needed to be. And that Keller bristled when he noticed Max's gaze.

"What are you doing?"

"Watching you," Max replied.

"Can you do better?" Keller pressed.

"I don't know, but I can try."

Max unfastened his apron and placed a square piece of trim wood underneath a plane, shaving the wood to smooth the plane and blend the pieces together. He crafted the slabs of wood for Keller to glue, readying the toy chest that Keller intended to give to his child for Christmas (or *Weihnachten,* what the Germans called December 25).

"Put the broom away," Keller said. "You're a pattern-maker now. But you have to work from blueprints."

Max started the next day.

He hadn't seen a blueprint in his entire life, but his mechanical mind helped compensate for inexperience. Max had a knack for finding the right angle quickly without meticulous filing. He'd soon analyze metal and wood parts to devise faster, more efficient soldering methods in his workshop. He learned to read and replicate the drawings well enough to make it in the Heinkel airplane factory pattern shop.

And Keller took a liking to Max. They weren't friends and certainly didn't engage in small talk. But Keller spared Max some of his rage. He would yell at others, break chairs in anger, beat laborers with the legs of those chairs when he deemed them incompetent. Sometimes Keller would kill laborers as a scare tactic.

But "he wouldn't touch me," Max says. "I either reminded him of somebody, or he saw the talent in me that I was that good with what I was doing."

●  ●

While Max was in Budzyn, two of his aunts labored in a munitions factory where they had been assigned following the Majdanek selection. Max had no idea at the time, however. He wouldn't even discover that they had survived until forty-two years later.

Max also didn't know what happened to Heniek and Fela after they were all separated at the Majdanek gates.

At first, Max didn't speculate much. He had plenty to process in Majdanek and Budzyn, and little nutrition to fuel creative thinking. Max focused on staying alive, avoiding the wrath of camp guards, and meeting labor demands.

"If you go into a 7-Eleven store and a gunman comes in with a gun, [your first thought is] where am I going to hide?" Max says. "You don't think of anything [else]—the fear knocks anything out."

But as Max settled into a routine at the shop, sometimes his mind wandered. Were Fela and Heniek among the lucky ones? Did some generous officer without children adopt Heniek and raise him as an Aryan baby? Did another take pity on Fela in the infirmary and decide to treat her and shield her from harm?

"It's an unknown factor," Max says. "You know [the Nazis] are going to do something bad. So when it first happens, it's like your child gets lost. Your bad thoughts never go."

At times, his wandering mind mustered some optimism. What was the downside to believing that God's hand had spared Heniek? Even after the war, Max would search for his brother, just in case he had been lucky.

Even in his nineties, Max retains a little curiosity and hope. He knows Heniek probably was killed in Majdanek; the gas chambers were difficult to evade. But how can he be sure?

"There was no closure, but there was hope that maybe they were alive," Max says. "If there's no closure, you cannot [give up hope]."

He didn't accept the deaths of his immediate family as absolutely certain, instead focusing on his determination to survive and what he calls the island of existence on which he lived. Metal springs, wooden squares, and blueprints became Max's new companions. How thick should the metal be to balance the spring back and create a perfect square? What slant should he cut the pattern on, and should he determine that slant by size or feel? How could he most efficiently shave the bulletproof laminated plywood?

"Just like an innovative thing I did to make everything faster," he says of a system he devised with washer and router.

Max had proven himself valuable to the war labor efforts. These skills would soon punch his ticket out of brutal Budzyn.

— • • —

In 1944, Keller was transferred to the Mielec labor camp and took a team of carpenters, including Max, with him. Max didn't know what month they went, but he estimates it was February or March based on the snow on the ground. A document he obtained after the war supports that guess, saying he was a carpenter in Budzyn for ten months before transferring.

Unlike the slow, circuitous deportation route out of the Warsaw Ghetto, they completed this roughly 130-kilometer trip from Budzyn to Mielec in a day. And Max believes Keller even arranged for Max to join him on a civilian passenger train, making the trip feel even faster.

"I don't know if I'm dreaming or not," he says when he thinks about the trip he spent sitting in a seat rather than crammed among bodies dead and alive. "It's real vague in my mind."

Max knows that a prisoner traveling by passenger train would have been highly unusual. But he remembers boarding a three-tiered transport when Mielec suddenly needed more labor.

"What makes me remember is also when you rode on a train there was a first-class wagon, then a two and a three," Max says. "And I remember riding on the three, third class, with Keller. It wasn't a long train ride."

The nine hundred inmates traveling were even gifted straw for bedding and bread, cheese, and water for nourishment. They arrived at Mielec to the usual procedure of delousing, threats, shaving, and a change of clothes. The camp doctor, Dr. Mosbach, and a German soldier added a new step to the intake process, however. In addition to having a prisoner number sewn on their clothes, each prisoner at Mielec was also tattooed with the letters "KL": *koncentration lager* (labor camp).

Max remembers the fear of being tattooed. Dr. Mosbach used a single needle to etch the first letter of each German word. The two letters were simpler than the string of numbers etched on the prisoners at death camps.

But where to tattoo the now-sixteen-year-old pattern maker? Max says he was the first in his group to receive the tattoo, and that Mosbach and his team were mulling over the proper placement.

They debated tattooing his forehead, pressing an inkpad to it— maybe as a scare tactic, Max wonders. He thinks they decided his forehead didn't offer a broad enough skin canvas. Dr. Mosbach instead settled on the bottom of Max's right wrist, crudely poking around until the needle penetrated.

"Very painful," Max says. "But you couldn't cry. There was very little that you could do."

"KL" became a tattoo for life, in more ways than one. Work it said, and work he did.

As Max settled in, he found Mielec was less brutal than Budzyn.

"Bad things," he encountered there, "but not as horrible as in the first camp."

Fewer hangings by the legs, the tactic that really shook Max. No more disemboweling, like at Budzyn when Max had seen "everything from the inside cut out," he says. "And it's just so gruesome that I don't even want to repeat it."

Mielec was more diverse. Barracks had windows, not just roofs. Bunks were stacked three high instead of four. Laborers included Poles, Germans—even some free workers—in addition to Jews. The commissioned laborers occasionally offered Max and his fellow slaves their sandwich leftovers, a welcome improvement from the bread-and-broth slave rations that were sparse and revolting. Mielec laborers received burned wheat coffee in the morning with their food. They hadn't had this amenity at Budzyn; but even so, the Mielec "coffee" tasted so bad, Max wouldn't touch coffee again for fifty years afterward. He came to tolerate it in the 1990s, he says, but only with a generous scoop of chocolate.

<hr />

In the carpentry shop, Max shifted from blueprints to pattern machinery after a confused fellow prisoner struggled to operate the system and severed his finger. A Nazi officer stepped on the detached finger and slipped. The officer then assigned Max the necessary grading, cutting, and planning. "Real huge machines," Max says. Mielec's factory was bigger than Budzyn's. But both supported the German war efforts.

Max's team worked on double-engine Heinkel bombers and single-engine Messerschmitt planes. Sometimes they'd work with a tail part; other times it was the cockpit or an aluminum crankcase to hold oil. He used chisels and hammers and handsaws and Plexiglas. He built parts with strengthened aluminum. Everything needed to be strong enough to withstand thousands of pounds of pressure. Any time Max completed a project, he'd put his assigned worker ID number, 14732, on the product. Everything needed to be perfect—redone to make it perfect, if necessary—to pass inspection. Max says consequences for faulty production ranged from isolation, to twenty-five lashes, to death.

"This is the kind of fear that you lived in," he says.

During moments when he could think clearly enough, Max wrestled with moral unease.

"I felt guilty, to a point, that I was helping the Germans," he says. "But I couldn't sabotage them because I had to put my number on [each part].

"At least it saved my life."

# CHAPTER 9

# "I did many things"

Mielec wasn't Budzyn, but it was still rough.

Nazi soldiers would march Max's group of laborers from barracks to factories, requiring them to sing while maintaining the same cadence. They were punished if they didn't. Max found the Ukrainian guards more vulgar than the high-brow Germans. The Ukrainians required prisoners to sing dirtier songs. They were more inclined to stab a prisoner who flubbed the lyrics.

Laborers worked section by section through the morning before "lunchtime": perhaps a slice of bread and watery soup. Bathroom breaks depended on SS guards' timelines, not prisoners' bladders. The factory bathrooms were fancy, Max says, but prisoners could only use outhouses.

"To this day, some of us don't have too much regularity because we had to wait," he says. If anyone went missing on a bathroom trip, others were killed to deter future escapes.

Max rarely missed work but remembers two times when he did.

Once, a Polish worker—was he angry? antisemitic?—threw a metal file, the sharp end piercing a hole in Max's back. Max dipped in and out of consciousness, afraid he was suffering from blood poisoning. He couldn't work for days and hid in the barrack, hoping the Nazis wouldn't find him unfit to work and kill him. A fellow inmate helped tend to Max as best he could. Sterile urine (Max's) was the best disinfectant, but Max couldn't reach the wound to clean it himself. So this stranger, whose name Max never learned, helped scrape off the cut. The inmate applied compression with a cloth soaked with the sterile urine to clean the wound. The teamwork enabled Max to keep the laceration a secret from the Nazis.

"I don't even remember how, why, and where," Max says of the stranger's kindness. Did he find Max because he was assigned an internal job in the barracks? Was the man a long-lost friend of Isaak's? What was his name, even?

The man hid Max from view when the Germans entered the barrack for inspection. Eventually, Max healed and returned to the factory.

Another time, Max volunteered to learn welding, as the Nazis baited prisoners with milk and extra food for mastering another useful trade. Max watched the electro-welding without protective glasses, leaving his vision spotty. He missed a day of work then too, but he soon healed.

◆•●

Max's memories of the camps oscillate between crafty survival tactics and moments of near despair. Pain too, though he tries to push the worst whippings from his mind. He blistered from the lashes he received but shed no tears, he says.

"My pain tolerance is very, very high. Some people cry over spilled milk.

"I think you survive better if you just place it in the 'life's experience' section."

Max would rather marvel at the time he smuggled a loaf of bread during one of the nighttime unloading chains, when prisoners carried bulk food shipments from boxcars to mess halls. The unloading stretched three, four, sometimes five straight hours. As rations passed from hand to hand, Max tried to calculate the likelihood that a guard would realize that one loaf among so many had gone missing; the likelihood that a guard would spot, in the dark of the night, that one prisoner on the long assembly chain was acting out; the likelihood that a single loaf, flung quickly into the bush behind the assembly line for later retrieval, would arouse attention.

He calculated, and he did it.

"I would hide it," Max says. "I don't know if anyone else did, but I know I did. I did many things…"

Another inconsistent but prized food source: kitchen assignments. Max doesn't remember what in the German mess hall needed fixing. Maybe a broken table leg. Keller assigned Max the job.

After Max completed the job, the kitchen staff rewarded him with leftovers: potato peelings they otherwise would have thrown away.

Max took scraps back to his workshop, fashioning a piece of metal between two electrical wires with which to cook the potato peels. Another time, he brewed coffee with the homemade appliance.

"We concocted some things," he says slyly.

He wouldn't let bunkmates know.

This wasn't the Warsaw Ghetto, where Max smuggled items both in and out of the walls to help himself and his family. Food was a precious commodity then, but even more so now. And in the camp, Max trusted no one. He didn't have friends, he says, because it was too risky. Times were desperate. Everyone fended for themselves, some betraying their fellow inmates to the guards if that was what they needed to do in order to survive.

In fact, Max remembers a bunkmate—an older man, around his father's age—once stealing a piece of bread Max had saved overnight.

"Acts such as that kind made it impossible to get close to people," Max says. "It's just a tragedy, and you just become so hardened that you beware anything."

Max now thinks the extreme encounters made him a good judge of people, perceptive of character while also intent to become a better person after escaping the suffering. And yet, he says, he'll always feel different. As adjusted as he would become to America and his postwar life, he's still a little suspicious after seeing the depths to which man will sink. Those trust-destroying years took place at a pivotal age; he transitioned from childhood to adulthood in the death and labor camps, and even his childhood friendships were marred by the disruption of the ghetto. At times, when he thinks he's being tricked or treated unfairly, his camp defiance instincts crop up. He gets feisty.

"I went from a child to an adult overnight," Max says. "It made me a hardened individual.

"I do have a heart, and I do have feelings—but very controlled feelings."

More than seventy-five years later, he sometimes welcomes company, but other times turns inward and distances himself.

"You get flashbacks," he says.

———— • • ————

Before liberation, the Nazis moved their prisoners west several more times, away from the approaching Allied armies. Onboarding processes differed. Max remembers some prisoners rushing to water hydrants to quench their thirst, but instead of being refreshed, they would unknowingly overwhelm their retracted stomachs and die.

Max moved from Mielec to southwest Wieliczka, a subcamp of Krakau-Plaszow near the city of Krakow. Keller didn't make the trip. Max heard "through the grapevine" of camp rumors that Keller returned home to care for his family after a 1944 bombing of Frankfurt am Main. Again, Max doesn't know the timing; he long thought he left Mielec in the fall of 1944, but more likely it was several months earlier, in the late winter or spring that year, as documents obtained by the American Red Cross show that he was out of Mielec by August.

Either way, it was on an open-roofed boxcar to Wieliczka where Max says he heard bombings for the first time since Warsaw. He wondered who was bombing whom.

The Nazis kept Max's group in Wieliczka only a couple of weeks, not even assigning them labor posts in the overcrowded camp. Wieliczka was like "a field of bodies," Max says, with too many people to feed or even to organize into a work facility. Rumors circulated wildly. There was plenty of time to worry about what would befall them next.

"To be perfectly honest, I don't know [what we thought]," Max says. "Being in a place that's new and not knowing what your fate is..." He shakes his head.

"Sometimes, when you live under conditions like that, your mind doesn't work normally either. What we think about right now, the analyzing that we do now, was nonexistent."

Before long, Max was back on a train to Plaszow's main camp with 2,700 other bodies who were barely alive but alert for the seventy-five-kilometer ride. Some historians believe the train even stopped at the death camp of Auschwitz-Birkenau. For some reason—maybe the sheer number of people already in the camp—the Nazis didn't unload their prisoners there. Max is glad they didn't.

# CHAPTER 10

# Between Right and Wrong

I nstead, for the first time, Max was transported to Germany.

According to a certified letter Max would obtain upon a return trip in 2016, Max first arrived at Flossenbürg on August 4, 1944. The same records confirm that Max was among "inmates who were in Concentration Camp Flossenbürg after 6 March 1944." One says Max was born May 14, 1926; the other, June 14, 1926. But the Nazis didn't know their young patternmaker was actually sixteen years old, not eighteen. They did know to leave blank the column for "date of death." Max's row is one of the few without a scribble denoting date and place of death. As with Budzyn, Mielec, and Wieliczka, Max would survive Flossenbürg.

Max remembers the August 4 arrival near the Czech-Austrian border, the train of prisoners color-coded by imprisonable offense. He was surprised at Flossenbürg's modern amenities, with barracks built from brick instead of wood, neatly arranged in the shape of an "L." Quarters for female slaves—sex slaves—stood to the right of the hilly grounds as the prisoners entered. A mess hall lay just beyond, the garbage cans behind it a popular spot to rummage for food scraps, Max would learn.

Then came a valley with crematoria. Signs at the camp today call it "Death Valley."

Flossenbürg was the most organized camp Max had seen, and the most diverse: Romani peoples (pejoratively called Gypsies), homosexuals, and political prisoners labored alongside Jews. Priests in their black robes and crosses roamed the grounds. Insignias on apparel denoted why each laborer was imprisoned here. Jews didn't wear the yellow Stars of David they had donned in ghetto days. They were classified as political prisoners and marked with an upside-down red triangle. Max wondered if prisoner diversity would mean improved treatment.

No such luck. "The Jews were still treated like the Jews," he says, "and the others were treated differently. You were still singled out as a Jew." Jews were still harassed, treated as scapegoats by other prisoners who would tell them to "get out of my way" or "I wish they had gotten rid of you." Jewish punishment was the most severe. Max remembers hangings and beatings—twenty-five lashes given to one hanging man who was falsely suspected of pilfering from the mess hall.

Flossenbürg was also the first camp at which Max had seen women after selection. In fact, women constituted roughly sixteen thousand of the ninety-seven thousand prisoners at Flossenbürg across its nearly one hundred subcamps over seven years. While there, however, all Max knew was that he—and all male inmates—were forbidden from talking to the women. Max wondered how long Flossenbürg officers let women live and to what tortures, exactly, they were subjected. The little he learned of why the guards selected them, what he calls their "immoral purposes," horrified him.

"Hearing a story like that just makes you lose a lot of faith in the human race," Max says of the rampant rape and sexual assault. He compared the horror to the shame he felt when his mom and aunts were disrobed and searched at ghetto's end.

"At my age, this was more destructive to me than some of the killings," he says. "It was the thing between right and wrong."

At Flossenbürg, Max received a shower, a change of clothing, and a barrack assignment. He no longer worried showers were actually gas chambers.

"We were doing jobs," Max says. "You were maybe not too valuable, but a valuable commodity. We were helping."

A typical day in Flossenbürg: Wake up before sunrise to lights that were suddenly switched on and shouts of "Get up!" Put on whatever makeshift clothes you were granted upon arrival to the camp, perhaps a shirt, a pair of pants, and in the wintertime, a jacket. Caps and socks were hard to come by, not to mention targets of theft if you did have them. Wooden clogs made do as shoes. Sometimes, Max would wash his hands and face in snow, rubbing his hands together to create heat.

They would then head to morning roll call for fifteen to twenty minutes of counting. Bunk searches ensued when a sick or oversleeping inmate threw off a count. Mess hall was next, where inmates each received a cup of burnt wheat coffee. March to work, in lockstep, singing. Again, officers often demanded that the inmates sing dirty songs.

"Some of them were nice songs," Max chuckles. "Others were not."

He declines to elaborate on the details of what he says were awful sexual lyrics: "Most of them were really horrible, and I just kind of don't want to repeat them."

By 7:30 or 8 a.m., Max estimates, they were at the Messerschmitt airplane factory in the complex. They'd keep laboring until a whistle signaled lunch hour. Like in previous camps, lunch hour didn't guarantee lunch. The only food was an occasional saved ration or gift from a laborer; Max would even eat that covertly in the outhouse, for fear he would be accused of having stolen it.

Through the afternoon they would work, slave laborers alongside civilian carpenters and patternmakers and engineers. Again, some nights Max's group would help unload provisions from the boxcars, shoveling potatoes, carrots, vegetables, and thousands of loaves of bread into burlap bags—a human chain of hundreds.

Whenever work finished, laborers returned to their barracks, sometimes washing off under a hydrant outside the bunk. Dinner was a piece of bread—about a twentieth of a loaf—and a bowl of soup, "dispensed nicer" than previous camps' soups. The water to vegetable ratio varied.

Some inmates used utensils; others drank the soup. Knives weren't distributed, but some laborers smuggled steel blades from their workshops to light fires in the bunk. They collected wooden chips and scavenged the trash for paper to generate flames inside metal drums. No one complained about a smoky bunk in exchange for reprieve from the freezing winter of the German mountains.

After dinner, inmates prepared for bed. Scuffles broke out occasionally, but Max tried to steer clear. Some inmates chatted or prayed. Max remembers looking up to older Jews who prayed by heart.

"I had all the respect in the world for them," he says. "Even through all the things they were going through and the way they were treated, they still had faith in God." Max communicated with God in his own words.

"Somebody listened because I'm here," Max says. "I'm a strong believer in that." His will to live didn't waver.

By 9:30 or 10 most nights, he says, the prisoners were in bed. Some prayed or sang, recited poetry, or said the foundational Jewish prayer, *Shema*. Max hummed, as he always had—and as he still does.

"We were still human beings," he says.

---

## Flossenbürg, 1944

Max remembers the dark-rimmed glasses, the suit, and tie. They didn't belong to a guard, but the foreman of Flossenbürg Barrack 11 had authority. He directed the young inmates climbing the barrack steps to the bunk they'd sleep in.

"I would like you," he told Max, "to sleep in this room with me."

The foreman pointed to a private section of the barrack. Unlike the bunks lining the barrack, the bed in this room had a mattress. Max felt special, granted a privilege. He figured a good night's sleep awaited him.

"I never considered that a person of his stature would not do it for the goodness," Max says. "I thought it was a kind deed, and I was happy he singled me out for that.

"Evidently, he did it to appease himself."

Why wouldn't sixteen-year-old Max assume the best? He credited kindness from authority figures like Keller as the reason he was alive and laboring. And Max had never received formal sexual education in school, the ghetto, or the camps.

"We didn't know the facts of life," Max says. "In the Jewish religion, we were brought up where everyone got their lips closed."

Max's memory has blocked out the night that followed. He doesn't remember details about the next morning, either.

Was he drugged? Given a drink? Did the foreman abuse Max in his sleep?

Other Flossenbürg inmates selected for that special room were raped, he'd learn sixty-nine years later on his first trip back to the camp.

With that new information, Max began feeling what he calls a "slight" sense that something went wrong that night in Barrack 11. Maybe that's why sexual references on television shows and in pop culture have stung ever since.

"When it involves sexual things, I maybe tear up or it triggers," he says. "I think he abused me."

Sexual exploitation and homosexual rape were common in Flossenbürg, where labor forces included prisoners incriminated for sex offenses. Max remembers another painful moment he didn't discuss for nearly seventy-five years, when three older men in his barrack preyed on a young laborer. The whole barrack was ordered outside as a result.

Teens like Max weren't safe in their bunks.

For decades afterward, Max felt shame. Could he confirm whether he was raped or sexually abused? Even if a physical test could tell him, he doesn't want to know. Believing the foreman meant the best helped him cope in camp. The man was acquitted in a postwar criminal trial.

Now, Max still struggles to articulate how he processed the traumatic night. He pauses when asked, stuttering over the word "embarrassing" even as he knows he should shoulder no guilt if he was a victim of abuse.

He worries what his kids would say if they knew the truth. Will his friends and family accuse him of lying for not sharing earlier? Max launches into a diatribe on the emotions—like sympathy—that he feels he never properly grasped after camp life.

Women coming forward with abuse allegations during the #MeToo movement helped empower Max to share his story. He hopes speaking out will dissuade potential sexual predators.

"You see in public that many women now are doing that, so it's an embarrassed…" Max stops midsentence. "Then you get to a point where you take account of your life and say, 'If I don't mention it, then nobody will know it and somebody's going to do it. Maybe this will prohibit someone else from doing it.'

"I'm really glad that it comes out, because it probably makes me feel easier."

# CHAPTER 11

# Where Are We Going?

## Flossenbürg—Monday, April 16, 1945

"All the Jews out!"

Max remembers jumping off the bunks and throwing on clothes when the Nazis woke everyone in his barrack at 5 a.m. sharp. The guards marched the Jewish laborers 3.7 miles to the nearest train station, where steam locomotives awaited them. They separated the 1,700 fugitives into groups of one hundred and assigned eight guards to each group. Then they boarded trains bound south toward the concentration camp of Dachau. But the trains wouldn't make it that far.

The day before, Max Koegel, the Commandant of Flossenbürg, had ordered prisoners to wait in their barracks rather than report for work on Sunday. At 3 p.m., Koegel assembled them all in a camp square. He separated the Jews. The next morning, they were out of the camp and on trains.

Now Max was crammed aboard a boxcar with roughly seventy others. He didn't know what to expect.

Suddenly, around 10:30 a.m., a stream of .50-caliber bullets pierced the wooden walls of the train, interrupting Max's thoughts. The train was passing through the nearby town of Floss when the bombardment began. Fighter planes aimed bullets at the open doorways. They killed Jews and some of the German officers standing guard at boxcar doors. Max saw one bullet pierce a man's back and dig into his backside, feces oozing out of his corpse. Another bullet ricocheted off a wall and decapitated a crouching passenger. The severed head rolled onto Max's lap, but he stayed calm as the man's red blood flowed over him; the blood later turned black. It was horrifying, but Max made himself focus on survival. He wasn't glad someone else got injured instead of him, but he thanked God he was still alive. The guards continued to yell: "Do not get off the car! Anybody who gets off the car gets shot!"

Max knew he could be shot on the car too. He didn't know by whom. He wondered whether the Allies responsible for the air raid were American or British (as he later learned, they were American). He deduced from their swastika-free flags that they weren't Nazis.

The trains halted until that evening. After the dead bodies were unloaded, the train resumed its travel through the night. Still, the guards gave their prisoners no food. Only on Wednesday did SS guards distribute four loaves of bread to each wagon. Any prisoner still alive was granted a tiny piece of margarine, according to later historical accounts.

The trains made it to Schwarzenfeld before a heavy strafing on Friday. Again, the planes seemingly "came from nowhere," Max thought, the loud trains disguising their approach. But this time, the American planes flying alongside the transport would destroy the trains completely. With machine guns everywhere, Max and the crew knew they needed to jump.

"It was more like a natural instinct," Max says. "Even the guards worried about their own life, so they just didn't do anything about it. They were in no position."

Max jumped from the boxcar. He saw other passengers do the same. Guards still warned inmates not to jump, but they knew they were fighting for their own lives too. It was the first time Max felt like he and fellow Jews might have an even fighting chance.

On his jump, Max landed face down in a ditch, a stray railroad conveyor belt to his side. A bullet ricocheted off the belt piece, the hot metal brushing the inside of his left leg. At first, he just felt a burn. He got up from the ditch and kept walking. Then he looked down and found a roughly 1.5-inch hole that the .50-caliber bullet had dug into his inner thigh. Blood gushed out.

"My first thought," Max says, was "'how do I stop the bleeding?'"

His overriding thought decades later: the bullet hit "just below my instrument—thank God."

Max tore fabric from the bottom of his shirt, creating a tourniquet that he double-knotted above the gash. The blood continued to flow. Max tried not to walk too awkwardly, afraid his impediment would attract German attention. Even after the strafing, officers around him were shooting and killing prisoners whom they deemed too infirm for the trek to come. The stench of decaying bodies was so strong that the German farmers who lugged the wagons of corpses wore gas masks. Prisoners who lugged adjacent wagons of Nazi equipment were not allowed that luxury.

Max was among a group the SS hurried into the nearby forest. He clutched his tourniquet as he began what would become known as a death march. Marching columns were two hundred men deep, heading southeast. They traveled at night to avoid discovery by Allied reconnaissance planes.

Eventually, the makeshift bandage successfully clotted Max's wound. It stuck to his leg. Max ripped it off, triggering a fresh flow of blood. He urinated on the wound to cleanse it, then wrapped a new tourniquet. He didn't want to become the latest corpse piled on the hay wagons.

Max saw farmland as they marched, then a dirt road to the forest where the prisoners were given time to rest. The prisoners subsisted on beets, grass, and potatoes from fields along the way. Max remembers pulling beets out of the ground himself. Then it rained. That night, Max thought the bodies seemed to pile especially high.

The torrent became so heavy that the guards let the muddy, rainy survivors take shelter in a barn in Stamsried. Lice festered as their wet clothing mixed with hay. Buckets of red beets were welcome nutrition. They continued across the forest to Neunburg vorm Wald through the weekend.

## Monday, April 23, 1945

Finally, a town, Max thought. A town square, a church—but here the guards lined up the survivors on the streets as villagers from nearby Neukirchen-Balbini spat on them. Max was among a crew ordered to drag a hand wagon of provisions and ammunition up a hill. By afternoon, they reached the hilltop. Forests sprawled beneath, where Max could just make out people running from the towns to the woods. He saw guards frantically ditching the swastikas on their shoulders and caps.

"Listen, all you Jews!" an officer blared over a speaker in German.

Lie down, they were told. Don't move. You're surrounded by machine guns and weaponry. If you move, we'll kill you.

One machine gun, Max says, was "real visible." Other machine guns, according to the guards, dotted the surrounding woods.

Then the guards retreated.

An hour later, some of the roughly six hundred survivors—Max's column plus another column they had bumped into and joined two days earlier at Neunburg vorm Wald—began to realize the guards had fled. They heard artillery fire and tanks coming from the town. Half of the survivors trekked onward from where they had traveled; the other half raced back to town. Max was among those who raced back. He wanted to be one of the first people the Americans liberated.

The same villagers who had just spat on them now rolled white bedsheets like flags of surrender to the Allied Forces. Some brought out buckets of milk for survivors to drink. General George Patton's 3rd U.S. Army tank division had arrived, although Max would not discover who they were until later. The English language and the American flag were both unfamiliar to him. He approached the tanks that distributed non-perishable foods and dehydrated proteins. One soldier handed Max a poncho to carry his rations in. And, as it happened, one set of papers that Max received from American liberators even documented that day as his birthday. It was fitting, Max says—freedom was like another birthday to him.

"We didn't know what it was or what to do," Max says of freedom. "That was my liberation."

He was 155 kilometers (ninety-six miles) away from the guards' intended destination, Dachau concentration camp. They had made it only fifty-eight kilometers (thirty-six miles) from Flossenbürg. Max didn't know those frames of references at the time, but he would learn much later in life that roughly 7,000 of the 9,300 evacuated Flossenbürg inmates died from exhaustion, starvation, or shooting along those marches. Of the 1,500 tattooed with Max at Mielec, only sixty-one survived long enough to be liberated.

Max was one of them. His sense of time and place, however, became muddled. Years of pain, starvation, and disarray stuck with him.

"Living that period of time without any nutritious value, you become brained," Max describes his foggy thoughts. "The way I use the bathroom, the way I eat with hunger—that sticks with you."

Max joined a group of about seven guys, he says, in a local house. He doesn't remember the full list of the seven but knows Jack Pollack, with whom he would stay friends in America, was there. So was an Isidore Meyerowitz, Leon Weiss, someone named Rice, and an older survivor who went by Apel. Their host didn't have rations, so Max went in search of food. He found a butcher shop in the alley behind his host's house. Max convinced the butcher in the bombed-out complex to donate meat to the newly freed teens. Their host then cooked the meat for them to eat. The whole effort was "done so spontaneous," Max remembers with his eyes closed, more than seventy years later. The house had pictures of a soldier on the wall, but he wore a German Wehrmacht military uniform rather than a Nazi one. Her son? Max wondered. He slept on the floor that night.

Max also pinched himself on this first day of freedom. He worried about his sudden independence. How would he find food and provisions? How would he achieve self-sufficiency for the first time in his seventeen years?

# RECLAMATION

# CHAPTER 12

# What Is Freedom?

Would they find real clothes, Max wondered? He felt like a wild animal.

He was wearing striped pants that carried him through the death march and a white shirt, still torn from when he crafted the tourniquet. The upside-down red triangle and his "14732" ID number were still sewn on the left chest of the shirt.

Max's cohort—was it five strong at this point? up to eight?—sought out the Amberg Bürgermeister, the chair of the town's executive council and the de facto town mayor. Could they just get one outfit each? Better, the Bürgermeister said. He found a shop owner and commissioned a suit and pair of shoes for each survivor. Max recalls vividly the seams down the middle of his first real pair of footwear in two years. And socks?

"The thing we didn't know about was socks," Max remembers, chuckling at the shirt fabric he'd torn to wrap around his blistered feet. "We still went around with a bandage-looking deal."

Max explored the Neukirchen-Balbini area for a few days, unsure which towns had been liberated and where the Americans had taken over. He and his friends knocked on more doors, hoping to find additional host families. The woman they stayed with the first night had been kind but didn't extend her offer a second night. She didn't mind their company, she told them, but she worried her neighbors would hurt her for harboring liberated Jews.

"Even if some of them wanted to do good, they had some people who didn't appreciate it," Max says.

Villagers set out bread and milk on their porches. Max was eager to take advantage of each kind gesture. One farmer distributed warm cider. But no one else offered beds. Villagers locked their doors, "for fear of what we might do to them," Max guesses. Even after liberation, he and fellow freed inmates slept in the wild.

They began hitchhiking along a highway. They'd heard farm roads couldn't take them to a city big enough to have accommodations. But where would they go even if they did find another urban center? And when they got there, what would they do next?

"We were just roaming," Max says.

They continued on like this until the U.S. Army 179th Signal Repair Corps pulled up in a jeep. A Jewish lieutenant named Bacic told Max and his friends they were in no condition to find a displaced-persons camp by foot. He loaded them into the three-quarter-ton truck behind the jeep. Max marveled at the portable stove aboard. Then there was the rush of riding in an automobile again.

"For five years, we'd never ridden in a truck or car," Max says. "It was overwhelming."

So too was Bacic's generosity. It was Bacic, Max says, who would show him what freedom meant. It was Bacic who clothed and fed them. It was Bacic who arranged for Max's infected bullet wound to finally receive proper cleaning and dressing from a Signal Corps medic at a temporary encampment in Schwabach.

Then, the corps headed for Nuremberg.

━━●◆●━━

# MAY 1945

Uniforms, food, a job? Max couldn't believe it. Lieutenant Bacic showed him to his room with eight other youngsters. Bacic offered them jobs helping the 179th Signal Repair Corps at Numeir Kabel Werke, a self-sustaining Bavarian Cable Works factory in Nuremberg where German POWs captured by the Allies labored over machinery. The factory was a "city inside a city," Max says, especially compared with the ghetto and camp confines where he had languished the last six years. Now he discovered a motor pool, bar, dance hall, and movie theater. Max could live with the soldiers, even wearing an American uniform without a prisoner insignia.

Max's mechanically-inclined mind shifted its energy from airplane pattern making to cooking. He trained initially under the lead mess sergeant. Then the sergeant, who was married, was caught smuggling coffee and food to a French girlfriend, Max says.

Just like that, Max became the lead mess sergeant for hundreds of German POWs, the resident Polish guards in charge of them, and occasionally American soldiers on the base. Max played billiards and ping pong with soldiers in the playroom, garnering a reputation as an avid "long-ball player" when he mastered the art well enough to twist serves. Was he finally reclaiming some of his childhood?

After the Nazis "took away the youth from us," Max marvels, "it was recreation."

But he took his duties seriously.

Max insists he had a special mess hall. He cooked a lot of soup, in a pot the size of a table, heated electrically or on gas stoves. He remembers the kitchen upgrades that helped him better feed the POWs. He organized kitchen shifts; German women whom the army had screened acted as servers.

Real-world food was a novelty. Butter, sugar, meat? Max hadn't enjoyed any in regular supply in nearly six years. Survivors needed to pace themselves when eating, as their bodies readjusted to normal nutrition. Max thinks he wasn't as malnourished as some survivors at liberation thanks to his crafty scavenging and solid build. He once estimated he was five foot four and ninety pounds after the death marches, but he never, before or after the war in European life, officially weighed himself.

"When you get sick and dwindle down, 'Oh, I'm going to get on a scale and see how much I weigh?' It's irrelevant," Max says. "And I was always athletic."

———•●•———

Max grins remembering the clever solutions he devised to salvage mess-hall challenges.

Sometimes, he made alcohol from scratch. He intricately explains how he used a five-gallon water bottle, thermos pot, and brass tube—how he would first ferment raisins and sugar and then add them to a boiling pot. Next, he would insert the brass tube into the boiling pot and fasten a thin, spiraled copper wire atop ice. The resulting steam and liquid, he says, was 100 percent alcohol. To make the alcohol last longer, Max would mix the strong liquor into half-empty cola bottles before doling them out to guards and POWs alike. He stashed away several cans. He would barter them for more kitchen ingredients.

Max bartered candy and cigarettes too, necessary in 1945, during a meat shortage when the American butchers went on strike. Max convinced farmers to sell him a live cow anyway. He recruited a Polish guard with butchering experience and the camp doctor, Lieutenant Mogil, to help.

"I brought in the cow, they slaughtered the cow, the doctor inspected the meat, and we were eating it," Max says. "This is the truth."

Another night, Max needed to prepare a banquet. The Numeir Kabel Werke staff was hosting a big-draw show with a visiting French dance troupe. What would Max cook for the crowd? He wanted to serve them goose, but he would need to find some first.

Max had only recently learned how to drive—just barely. In Nuremberg, a factory officer had showed him how to start a jeep (no key, Max learned) then set him free in a field with exploding bullets. Max tried to navigate that field, confused where the bullets were coming from. He learned later that when the war had ended, the Germans had stashed much of their artillery in a ditch near that field. The day Max first got behind the wheel, Army soldiers had decided to pour gasoline on the artillery and light it on fire. And thus, Max's first drive was among exploding bullets. He never took a formal lesson.

With that experience, Max revved up a 2.5-ton truck headed southeast toward a farm near Munich. He doesn't remember how exactly he bought or bartered for the geese but thinks the methods were illegal.

"So I have a truck with geese, and if you ever heard geese bock-bock-bock," Max says, you would know his ride back with the gaggle was raucous. He wondered if the police car he spotted behind him would pull over the suspicious cargo load. But the truckload made it back to the kitchen unscathed. A German POW stuffed every goose with flour to fatten them up. The day of the French dancer show, the geese were killed and cooked. Dinner was served.

# CHAPTER 13

# Wasted Time

Nearly seven months had passed since liberation, and Max wanted to be useful.

*Wants to find mother, but does not want to go back to Poland. Interested in mechanics. Now in transport of rations. A lot of his time is wasted.*

That's how a displaced persons recordkeeper summed up Max's life in the first postwar months, according to records he received in 2013. The records compiled on November 11, 1945 credit him with fluency in Polish, Yiddish, Hebrew, German, Russian, and English. Max laughs now at their definition of "fluent"—he had learned only basic vocabulary in the Warsaw Ghetto with little chance to speak English until liberation. The records also note that he contracted typhus during the war and that an uncle in Palestine was interested in taking him in.

Somehow, Max never learned the last piece of information—that a living family member was searching for the orphan—until he obtained the batch of records on a return trip to Germany in 2013. It was then that Max began to grasp the extent of the fruitless correspondence attempts he and his uncle Aharon sent one another in 1946 and 1947.

Max filed a search document for Aharon on August 3, 1946. Aharon filed an inquiry on October 4 through the Jewish Agency for Palestine's Search Bureau for Missing Relatives. The form asked what suggestion the relative had for the child's future.

"Wishes the child to come to Palestine," Aharon wrote from Haifa, "and is willing to assist and support him." But Max never got the message.

The documents reached the United Nations Refugee Rehabilitation Association's (UNRRA) Child Tracing Branch in December 1946.

"We have located an uncle of the above-named boy," reads a letter to the district child search and repatriation officer. "His name and address are Aharon HOFFMAN, Kvutzat, NEVE-EITAN, Post HAIFA, Palestine. The message received is 'wishes the child to come to Palestine and is willing to assist and support him.'"

A UNRRA welfare officer responded on January 2, 1947.

"We are sorry to inform you," the officer wrote to the Central Tracing Bureau, "that the above mentioned boy has never been in our center."

Later that month, Max, still in Nuremberg, used his broken English to file a search request for any living family member. The January 29, 1947 document reads:

> *Dear Sear:*
>
> *I am a DP from Poland. My name is MENDEL GLAUBEN.*
>
> *I am born in Warsaw 14 January 1928. I would like to get same information abaut my family (if its pasible)*
>
> *Here are the names of parsons I am loking for:*
> *FAIGA GLAUBEN. OR. FAIGA HOFFMAN.*
> *Born in Warsaw in 1907. Last so in Lublin concentration camp 1943.*
>
> *HENIEK GLAUBEN born in Warsaw in 1930. Last so in Lublin concentration camp 1943.*

*And if you know somthing about any pupils with
the name of GLAUBEN or HOFFMAN from Warsaw
pleas let me know*

*Thank you
Mendel Glauben*

*P.S. I have a ankel in Palestine with the name of
AHARON HOFFMAN. And I do not know hes
adres. The only thing I can remember is: Petach
Tikwa Palestine.*

*If you can give me same information about him. I
be very glad to hear about it.*

*Thank you again,
Mendel Glauben*

Max followed up on February 26, looking for uncle Aharon in
"Petach-Tikva or another place."

"Has the boy left your centre?" the Central Tracing Bureau acting
director asked on March 7.

Even before the ghetto walls had gone up, Hebrew lessons at *tarbut*
school had prepared Max for eventual immigration to Palestine. But Max
was never able to confirm in the 1940s that Aharon was alive. And Max
found Palestine, on the brink of its war of independence, unattractive.
He wasn't looking for another fight. He had already been embroiled in
more than a life's worth of conflict, he reckoned.

"I thought it was an undeveloped country, and there was fighting
going on," he says. "I just went through all this fighting and all this
ghetto. Let me live a little for a while. That's why I wanted to be in the
United States. It was a free country and a free society."

Max set his hopes on America.

In 1947, U.S. army servicemen arranged for Max to relocate to the UNRRA Aglasterhausen Children Center so he could apply to immigrate to the U.S. as an orphan. The catch: he needed to be younger than eighteen years old, and he was now nineteen. Enter another birth date for Moniek Max Glauben.

Max arrived at the center, he thinks, in late summer or early fall. He remembers playing his first organized soccer game there. He played back, defending right and left, and never let up a goal. Some girls he befriended studied with the woman who ran the orphanage, Rachel Greene. Max mostly worked in the kitchen but occasionally joined evening classes. They watched movies on a projector.

**Max (back row, third from left) pictured with fellow teenagers at an Aglasterhausen, Germany orphanage in 1947.** *Photo courtesy of the Dallas Holocaust and Human Rights Museum, Max Glauben Collection*

Around September or October, an opportunity arose. Would someone supervise three babies meeting with the immigration committee?

Mrs. Greene "came into the kitchen and wanted to know if I'd help them," Max says. "I was always helpful."

Mrs. Greene, Max, and the babies rode a three-quarter-ton truck to the American consulate in Stuttgart. Max never knew who the babies under his care were. He didn't know who many of the orphanage children, Jewish and non-Jewish, living with him were.

"Because many people were displaced, you understand," he says. "So when they were scattering the remnants of the leftovers, there were all [backgrounds of kids]. It could've been the Jewish babies born in the displaced persons camp."

Regardless, Max believes the sympathy they generated secured him an earlier ticket to the States.

The odds were against them: the U.S. accepted just 1,275 children between 1945 and 1948, under the Truman Doctrine, which granted preference to refugees and displaced persons within the national quota. But when the councilor saw the babies, Max says, he took pity and waived the quota.

Max had several advantages as an immigrant prospect. Thanks to American movies, American music, and conversations in U.S. Army kitchens, Max was now conversational in English. He knew how to drive and how to tinker with automobiles, as his caseworker would learn upon his arrival to the States. He was a highly recommended kitchen manager in the army, drawing praise for his ability to follow instructions. And Max was an eager worker; he recognized the value of his wartime contributions to airplane carpentry even as he regretted that his labor product supported the country that was imprisoning him.

Max received a permanent visa through the United States Committee for the Care of European Children, as well as immigration papers that noted his array of legal birthdays, his "Hebrew" religion, and his Jewish nationality. He had pretended to be older to avoid the crematoria at

Majdanek and later underreported his age to qualify for refuge in the Aglasterhausen orphanage amid immigration quota guidelines. The many birthdays would trickle through his legal documents for the rest of his life.

He was medically cleared and sent to a resettlement center in Stuttgart on November 20, 1947. The center's "nominal roll of authorized movement of displaced persons" lists 122 passengers of varying religions and countries. Polish, German, Czech, and Ukrainian passengers joined Max, the papers noted. Some passengers were classified as "stateless" and "stateless Jewish."

Beneath the 122 passengers' records—name, nationality, sex, age, identification card, and remarks—is a section of four additional passengers.

"The following children from Aglasterhausen," the document reads, "joined the group at Bremen."

The second of the four names is *"Glauben, Max. Polish-Jew. Male. 17. Aglasterhausen."*

This was authority enough for Max to board the S.S. *Marine Flasher*, a converted merchant-marine ship. The port of Bremen, Germany would be his last view of Europe for a decade. Displaced persons documents log his whereabouts differently, one accurately recording him on the "list of closed cases/children resettled to U.S.A." Another simply says Max "left for other area." A third—stamped in May 1955 and March 1957—records an erroneous destination for the young traveler.

The papers say, *"GLAUBEN Mendel, Born 14.1.28, is presumably gone to Palestine. Case closed in May 1948."*

Max—and later U.S. records—note the truth, though.

On November 27, Max Glauben was bound for the States.

# CHAPTER 14

# Sails Up

Max's first thought boarding the S.S. *Marine Flasher* was "I hope I make it."

The ship was smaller than he anticipated for a vessel slated to travel 3,200 nautical miles to its destination, but he found his assigned space among the triple bunks and hammocks. His ticket cost $142, per the U.S. Maritime Commission's alien passenger manifest form. Well worth his sponsor's cost, Max figured, as he sailed away from the Nazi horrors, away from life as a displaced person, away from the war-torn countries scarred by a murderous regime. Or at least that's what Max hoped.

On the shaky voyage, passengers struggled to keep their food down. Dining halls were mostly empty due to the pervasive seasickness. Max estimates he never saw more than six passengers in the dining hall at the same time. His stomach fared better than most. But then he sat near an older German man escorting a "youngster" to the States. The older man began shoveling sugar generously—was it five spoonfuls?—into his coffee. Max wondered how the man's concoction would jive with the rocky waters.

"I've made this trip over the ocean many times," the man told Max. "Don't worry."

He then took a swig of the coffee and sugar. The man threw up. Seeing the vomit, Max did too.

Nerves didn't help. Max felt excitement, anticipation, and joy at various points of the trip as his mind raced with fantasies of what awaited him in America. He was eager to discover adventure in the unknown. Germany was once unknown too, but Max came to delight in his mess hall responsibilities and recreational opportunities at Numeir Kabel Werke.

Max also thought back to *The Prince and the Pauper*, one of the American movies he'd seen in Germany after the war. He wondered which title character's life his American destiny would more closely resemble. Would America bring a life of luxury and splendor, or challenges he had never yet considered? Was it possible, Max wondered, that concentration camps and beatings and mass murders awaited in the States too? Even if he eluded torture, how would he find food and shelter, and a job or school? Would some generous American take Max under his or her wing like Lieutenant Bacic had in the days after liberation? What should a nineteen-year-old orphaned refugee do first to settle in a new country with a new language?

Questions and doubts swirled. Physically, he traveled safely on the S.S. *Marine Flasher*; but Max felt that psychologically, he had toppled overboard.

"Being orphaned without any relatives, that was not a full, complete freedom," Max says. "It was the equivalent of throwing you off the ship in the middle of the ocean and saying, 'Do all the getting to shore by yourself.'"

Max tried to refocus on the possibility of happiness and opportunity in America. He defined happiness as the stability his family enjoyed in Warsaw before Nazi occupation. He wondered if he could recapture that quaint time.

"It's just the unknown," Max says. "What could I dream of after being under bad conditions for five years? I forgot what the good things were."

As the fifteen days dragged on, Max distracted himself by watching games played aboard the ship. Cards were popular. During one game of poker, a passenger lost a dime while anteing on his face-down cards. Max's eyes darted to the shiny coin. He stepped on it as a search across the deck began. Max didn't budge.

"When [the search] was over, I bent over and picked up a dime," he remembers proudly. "So when I came to the States, I had a dime."

The dime, and a piece of British wool, were among Max's few belongings as the *Marine Flasher* approached New York Harbor on December 12, 1947. Max wasn't concerned about what he lacked when he first saw the country that awaited him. He couldn't take his gaze from the Statue of Liberty as he tried to wrap his mind around her enormous frame that welcomed him from a distance. He pointed, wide-eyed. As the *Marine Flasher* inched closer, Max says he felt like a "little pawn" beside Lady Liberty. Then he noticed her weather-worn imperfections.

"When you get closer, it's like life," Max says. "Like you yourself as a human being that the wind has knocked some of the paint off and the rain has gotten some of the color out, so not all the things are as real as they seem to be from far away. The closer you get to the subject, the better you could see it and the better you could solve it."

Max remembers thinking a paint job could "solve" Lady Liberty's rust. He wondered if he could solve whatever challenges lay ahead in America as easily. He'd have some help. A social worker—Max guesses someone from Jewish Children's Service, though he never knew—helped cover costs at customs when Max couldn't afford to pay for the right to carry in his British wool. She also guided Max to his next home: an orphanage on Caldwell Avenue in the Bronx, New York.

# CHAPTER 15

# Welcome to America

## December 15, 1947

Who was this alert, curious teen, anyway? He came from Germany, and before that from Poland, according to his immigration papers. But he spoke English quickly and with slang. His blue-green eyes were bright and lively; his blond hair was curly. A strongly built frame was evident beneath his G.I. clothing. No wonder he was so good at soccer, as his papers indicated. Max was worldly, and he wanted to go to a big city. He had a keen sense of business, which he attributed to his father's newspaper company that had dissolved a decade earlier. He had a keen sense of people too, which he traced to his mom's "unusual understanding" of her children. His parents had answered any questions he asked patiently, Max told E. Liebowitz of the Jewish Children's Service reception center. They had been gone four and a half years now.

If it hadn't been for the war, Liebowitz wrote in her case report, Max would have followed his father into the newspaper business. That would have made his father happy. Now Max had to do what he could by and for himself in America.

"I can accept direction and discipline," Max assured Liebowitz when she outlined the reception center's rules. But he wanted to know who might host him next: Was there a tolerant American Jewish family willing to take him in as he adjusted to his new surroundings? He had grown up religious, Max told the caseworker, but not fanatically so. He was bright, capable, and handy with machines. He hoped to master a trade in a burgeoning industry. After a first impression, Max wanted to stay in New York. But he knew that wasn't one of his resettlement options.

Liebowitz observed that Max was "alone and depressed." Still, he impressed her as an "intelligent, alert boy…well liked by the group." He was profoundly self-aware, able to understand and articulate the root causes of each feeling. As she explained in the case report:

*At present, he finds it a little difficult to concentrate over a long period of time. He is a little afraid of how this will affect his ability to study. He has enough insight to remark that this is probably due to some inner tension and nervousness about the future. He is successful, however, in hiding these feelings from people. He has often heard people say that he is one of the most stable and unharmed young men who has lived through the war experience.*

---

Max needed time to adjust to a country less deeply rooted in antisemitism. Police officers made him nervous at first. Would uniformed public servants still target him? His European style would surely attract attention, he worried.

"You stick out like a sore thumb," he remembers thinking to himself.

The longer he stayed in New York, the less he wanted to live there. Radio City Music Hall, Times Square, Coney Island? Max enjoyed them in the moment before realizing that the American kids he was seeing had been living a normal childhood and still had their parents, while he had been starving on a death march, an orphan. They danced, laughed, and enjoyed the sights. Max had no family, no home, no guarantees for the future. It was too much to swallow.

"I could not understand, and I became very depressed that I was confined for five years in the ghetto and…camps," Max says. "And while I was there, in another part of the world, there were kids dancing, there were people enjoying."

Sure, Max was intrigued by an RKO Pictures Christmas production featuring the Rockettes and pilgrims that seemed to fly in the air. Max liked skating and museums. Nightclubs fascinated him. He didn't like the bitter cold when New York experienced its worst blizzard since 1888 (26.4 inches of snow). And he didn't like "rough" New Yorkers.

Take the man in the Bronx whom Max asked for directions to the nearest pharmacy. The line was long at the first drug store Max had tried, so he looked for another soda counter.

"Do you see all the people around?" Max says the man barked back. "Why do you have to ask me?"

Retorts like that reaffirmed Max's growing suspicion that he wanted to leave New York for good, although decades later, he would come back for a hot dog from Nathan's and later a meal at Carnegie Deli.

For now, though: Where would Max go? Who would take him in?

The answers surfaced quickly. Just a week after Max met with Ms. Liebowitz, Jewish Children's Service had finalized arrangements with a Miss Marcuse. By December 28, they were planning Max's departure from New York. On December 30, Max had his itinerary.

---

## December 31, 1947

Max boarded an Eastern Air Lines flight from New York wearing a destination tag on the chest of his suit that read "Atlanta, GA," then waited through a layover in Washington, D.C. He had spent so many days and months designing airplane parts during the war, but Max had never before boarded a plane. The ride was "like a novelty," he says. "It was like the magic carpet." He still has the ticket stub.

Max says he wasn't scared to ride in the plane. But he was slightly alarmed when, all of a sudden, he couldn't hear the passenger next to him talk anymore.

"I didn't panic," Max says, "but couldn't figure out why I didn't hear."

A stewardess came to his rescue with a small white square that Max thought resembled a pill. He stroked curiously its hard outer shell as the stewardess mimed a chewing motion with her cheeks. Max began to chew the minty substance that he learned was called "gum" in America. He would also learn what it meant for his ears to pop.

Max was tired and fighting a slight cold when he landed in Atlanta. A caseworker met him at the Piedmont Hotel to take him to a foster home run by Mrs. Rosenthal.

Mrs. Rosenthal greeted Max in what he would come to know as her "usual motherly fashion," including the first home cooking he would eat in nearly a decade. Then Isidore Meyerowitz, whom Max was with at liberation and in Nuremberg, walked in, and the boys reunited enthusiastically. Max met Mrs. Rosenthal's son, Morris, and one of the wards, Saul Weintraub. Saul told Max, "It's New Year's Eve, and I'm taking you to a party."

Then Saul sauntered off to another party and left Max—who knew neither his way around Atlanta nor Mrs. Rosenthal's address—behind. Two girls came to Max's rescue, however. They said they knew where Mrs. Rosenthal's foster home was. Join us for the midnight showing of *Romance on the High Seas*, they told Max, and then they'd arrange a ride home for him.

Max still vividly remembers Fox Theater on Peachtree Street.

"When we walk hand in hand," Doris Day sang on the big screen, "The world becomes a wonderland.

"It's magic…"

That night, at least, Max was happy.

# CHAPTER 16

# To Texas

## January 3, 1948

M ax surveyed the three suitcases that had arrived in Atlanta, remembering how he'd cobbled together these scattered belongings during the last two and a half years.

He'd collected two Army sweaters and one red sweater, one overcoat, and one leather jacket, his caseworker wrote down. Max also owned six worn European sport shirts, six pairs of shorts, six handkerchiefs, three undershirts, one sweatshirt, and a pair of pajamas. For fancier occasions, he had an old brown suit and a newer suit, what the caseworker described as a "Very European Suit." Max hoped the beige-checkered English tweed material he bartered for in Germany would one day become his newest suit. He could choose whether to pair each with his moccasins or black shoes.

A fountain pen, a wrist watch, a deck of playing cards, shaving equipment, and a Bible filled out the rest of the suitcases. The Bronx orphanage had given Max a pair of *tefillin*, a traditional Jewish religious article in which small scrolls of parchment are encased in black leather boxes, one for the arm and another for the head, each box connected to long leather straps. And Max had a Kodak camera that he had bartered for with cigarettes on the Nuremberg black market. "I was a wheeler-dealer," he says.

A caseworker gave Max three dollars plus checks for clothes and explained his options: he could register for work with the U.S. Employment Service or attend school. If he chose school, the Jewish Children's Service would pay his board for two months to help him get back on his feet. They had already sponsored a dental visit the day before, with plans for a physical at the doctor.

Max enrolled in a night school in Fulton County and then in a Georgia Tech engineering program in Chamblee, a northeast suburb of Atlanta. He passed the program's entrance exam, which was designed for military personnel returning from World War II. But the curriculum overwhelmed the young immigrant, who hadn't been formally educated beyond his early teens and who hadn't spoken English regularly until age seventeen. Max lasted only a few weeks once classes began, he estimates, before he decided that he should seek work instead.

"It was just too hard for me to do all this and do the work and try to be sane," Max says.

Besides, formal higher education hadn't been his goal upon reaching America. He decided it would be more realistic to prioritize finding a stable job after so much tumult in his young life. The job search began.

First, Max trekked to a Sears and Roebuck department store. He asked if he could speak to the employment manager.

"He's busy," a woman working there replied.

"I'll stay here until he's free," Max insisted. He waited all day, begging for work when the manager emerged mid-afternoon. Max landed a job in the packing department, organizing mail orders for flooring, tiles, knives, and more. He worked as much overtime as Sears and Roebuck would grant. He began earning his keep.

"I was a go-getter," Max says. "I cared for myself."

In the months that followed, Max became the top salesman of economy shoes at Edward's Shoe Store, and he even taught the foxtrot and tango at Arthur Murray Dance Studio.

"I was just a layman," he says of the dance skills he had cultivated on German dance floors, "but did it my style, and people liked it."

By 1950, Max and his friend Al Zomper decided to open a grocery store. Max had the savings to buy the storefront; Al had grocery experience. They ran A&M Supermarket until they were called to serve in the U.S. Army in 1951.

Max had registered with the Army three years earlier, when he was eighteen years old, according to his American papers (or twenty, his real age). He didn't mind; he was grateful for the freedom and safety America had provided, and he wanted to give back in return. When he and Al were drafted, they sold the store to a couple who had recently emigrated from Europe. Max began basic training in Fort Hood, Texas; Al, in Alexandria, Virginia.

**Max at Fort Hood circa 1951–53.** *Photo courtesy of the Dallas Holocaust and Human Rights Museum, Max Glauben Collection*

After basic training, Max applied his experience as a mess sergeant in Germany to food service school in Fort Hood. He graduated as an honors student, he recalls with great pride, and rose through Army ranks. Within a year, he was promoted from private to corporal to sergeant to staff sergeant.

"At first I was promoted real fast," Max explains, "because the company had to be full strength before they ship out to Korea. But they never did, so I stayed stateside."

One weekend during his Fort Hood training, Max met Al for a weekend trip to Dallas. He never expected what came next.

# CHAPTER 17

# Frieda "Stubborn"

F rieda Gappelberg wasn't really doing anything that Saturday night in 1951.

So when her friend Gertrude Fair—"Trudy" to all her friends— invited Frieda over to meet a couple of servicemen, Frieda agreed to meet them on Park Row. Then Frieda, Trudy, Max, and Al went bowling.

Trudy and Al had already been dating. Frieda wasn't sure what to make of Al's friend; she only knew that the Fairs had taken him in like one of the family.

But Max knew what he made of Frieda. He continued to ask her out anytime he could get leave from the Fort Hood base, 157 miles southwest of Dallas. They bowled, they saw movies, and they went dancing. Danced and danced some more. That Max does have rhythm, Frieda thought.

Sometimes, Max stayed with the Fairs, who continued to treat him like a son. Other times, he stayed in a hotel near the Pocahontas Street Jewish Community Center (JCC), which hosted Jewish servicemen each weekend.

"I consider myself lucky because I was never a stranger because I was Jewish," Max says. "The same things that I was persecuted for by the Nazis."

The JCC also organized Saturday night dances for servicemen to meet Dallas girls. Sunday, the servicemen enjoyed breakfast at the center before returning to their bases. In the year to come, Max and Frieda attended several events, dancing at the JCC, the drive-in restaurant Louann's, and at the dance club Pappy's. Frieda was thrilled to find such an adept dance partner.

"Oh God, yes," she says, "I think that's one of the things that drew me."

But some dates went better than others. Max worried when they didn't go well. He tried to leave his concerns on the base when he came to Dallas. That was sometimes difficult, however. Once, the chance that he would be deployed distracted Max so much that he wrote to Frieda apologizing for how their last date had gone.

The letter, dated January 16, 1952, starts simply enough.

*I told [my superior] I was writing a letter to a cute little girl and also waiting for the ration. He said that since she is cute he won't disturb me any longer.*

Then Max turns serious, even vulnerable.

*Well I am going to start from the beginning. I have enjoyed myself last week, but not as much as a week before. I know it wasn't your folt it was mine. I had quite a few things on my mind and I thought that I was getting away from them but I didn't. One of those things was that they picked out 25 men to go to Korea. And I did[n't] know if I was on the list. But they told me Monday when I got back that I wasn't on it. And that fixed me up all right. But who know's for how long? And that is one reason why I wasn't feeling to good last weekend.*

*I really would like to go there [Dallas]. And take you out ice skating and maybe you will be able to proof to me how good of skater you are.*

*You better be better than I am.*

*Well that's all the news up till now. I only ask myself why I would get stationed a little closer to Dallas so I would be able to see you more often. Because I really miss you up here.*

They dated for a little longer. Then Frieda changed her mind about seeing him.

"I decided it wasn't what I wanted—I have no idea why," she says more than sixty-five years later. "We just didn't jell at that time."

Max says he handled the rejection calmly.

"I wouldn't be here ninety years if I took everything that happened to me seriously," he says. "How many times do you want something and someone says no and then the next day they say yes?"

—◆•◆—

Thanks to Trudy Fair—Trudy Zomper, by that time—Max and Frieda's story didn't end in 1952. Trudy had moved with Al to the base in Alexandria. But they visited Dallas for New Year's Day, 1953. Max came to Dallas to see Al. Trudy implored Frieda to join them.

"Why don't you go out with Max?" Trudy asked her friend. "We can go out together."

Frieda hesitated. She had a date with another serviceman for New Year's already. She didn't believe in breaking dates.

"I was not the most popular girl in town," Frieda says. "When I had a date, I kept it."

Trudy convinced her to break the date anyway. Frieda says it was the first and only date she ever broke, and she and Max joined the newlyweds for New Year's. Max was still a great dancer, she recalls. Frieda began to remember why she had liked him in the first place. They kept seeing each other, even after Al and Trudy returned home. This time they didn't stop.

Frieda even began to accept Max's claims that she was stubborn. It was now her turn to fess up, in a letter from January 14, 1953—

Max's twenty-fifth birthday (or twenty-third, according to his U.S. identification).

> *Dearest Max,*
>
> *I know I said I'd wait till you wrote, but I kept thinking of you so I said "to heck with what I said" so, here I am.*
>
> *I'm getting your address from the letters I got from you last year at this time. I've only changed the P.F.C. (to) Cpl. I hope it's right.*
>
> *Well Max it seems like all have survived our spree of Saturday night. Trudy and I are back to normal and I've fixed her skirt and got mine back from the cleaners. Believe it or not, it looks better now than it did before the drink got all over it.*
>
> *Max, if I said anything foolishly Saturday night, please forgive me—it was all the drink and the wonderful evening. I had such a grand time and I hope you also had as nice a time.*
>
> *Do you know yet whether or not you're going to be restricted for the 3 weeks? I hope not!*

Frieda promises to send a picture to Max, and then wraps up the letter.

> *Well Max, I suppose this is about all for now. Do write real, real soon. Be good—*
>
> > *Love always,*
> > *Frieda "Stubborn"*
>
> *P.S. You know Max, I believe you—I am very, very stubborn.*
>
> *P.P.S. I mailed the letter you asked me to mail. Bye now—write soon.*

By May, Max had been discharged from active service and moved to Dallas. He brought with him the diamond he had purchased from an elevator salesman in Furth, Germany (and apparently hidden well enough to keep it from being noted in his immigration papers). At the time, Max had anticipated the diamond would serve as barter. Instead, he had it reset onto a ring and used it to propose to Frieda.

Max "wasn't that romantic," he insists, but Frieda said "yes" anyway. He would be the only boyfriend she'd ever have. Frieda was the only girl Max would spend much time with too. He was touched by how caring she was. Frieda liked that Max was kind, that he was good to her, and that he was Jewish.

**Max's June 18, 1954 certificate of naturalization.** *Photo courtesy of the Dallas Holocaust and Human Rights Museum, Max Glauben Collection*

"I'm not going to say there was true love in the beginning," Frieda says. "But I never regretted it."

Her family did. The Gappelbergs weren't outright rude to her fiancé, Frieda says. Her dad, a barber, cut Max's hair. But it took time before the Gappelbergs warmed to Max, and even then they warmed slowly. Frieda's not sure whether they knew Max had survived the Holocaust, but she says they definitely didn't know the details or even what it really meant. She didn't know much yet either, she admits. What Frieda did know was how her parents and brothers treated Max.

There was "just not a lot of extra love shown" by her parents Mose and Rose, nor by her brothers, Frieda says. Max sensed they didn't trust him.

"He's not for you," they told her bluntly, unimpressed that she had chosen an unsettled veteran who had neither a job nor a formal higher education.

Frieda thought the knock on Max's limited education was unfair; her brothers had neither stable jobs nor college degrees. Her parents didn't factor that in, she says.

"Basically, they just thought Max was not going to amount to anything," Frieda says. "And that I should do better.

"In the end, Max proved himself."

# CHAPTER 18

# The Car Ride

The wedding was simple. No major ceremony, nor the type of fanfare "girls dream of," Frieda says.

"I'm not a socialite" anyway, Max says of the small get-together.

An extravagant celebration "wasn't monetarily feasible, and my mother didn't have the knowledge to do it," Frieda says. "She was doing it the Polish way. That's the way it was."

They're not sure if anyone received a formal invitation.

A rabbi married Frieda and Max quietly in his study. A reception for friends and family in the Agudas Achim synagogue social hall followed. The Gappelbergs prepared the food themselves. A carved turkey, Frieda remembers. She wore a blue bridal dress instead of white. It's the only dress Frieda liked when she went shopping.

**Max and Frieda on their wedding day June 14, 1953.**
*Photo courtesy of Max Glauben*

The wedding day, like the marriage that would follow, had its ups and downs. Max and Frieda had rented a furnished apartment to retire to that night. Frieda fell sick and went to sleep instead. Neither is quite sure what Frieda knew about Max's Holocaust background at the time. Max had mentioned the war when it was relevant in conversation about current events, but he revealed no details about his personal experience. He was proud he was capable of driving and working in the States and had served in the U.S. military. Could these independent, normal American practices help Max redefine himself as a normal American, rather than a survivor, refugee, or immigrant? Perhaps his war memories would fade with time.

"Sometimes you say, 'Let bygones be bygones forever,'" Max says. "In those days if you told them, they wouldn't believe it anyway."

◆●◆

Max found a job in Dallas in the summer of 1953 working with blueprints again. This time, he designed brass piping instead of German warplanes. Frieda worked as a secretary, typing shorthand. She'd learned how to type on a typewriter her dad had given her.

They saved money for a honeymoon later that summer. Max's boss's sister had bought a motel on the water in Longboat Key, Florida and gave Max and Frieda a good deal. They rented a car and drove the 1,200 miles for a waterfront getaway.

Max's chief memory from the drive is his exhaustion at the end. But to Frieda, the drive was a pivotal moment in their relationship. She was half-asleep in the car, she recalls, when Max first started telling her stories from his concentration camp days.

"I knew he was a survivor, but they weren't talking about it," Frieda says. "That was the first time he really spoke of it, went into a little more depth."

Frieda's mind raced as Max explained the boxcar deportation from the Warsaw Ghetto, the separation from his mother and Heniek at Majdanek selection when they arrived. She remembers the first time Max told her about Isaak pulling Max's arm toward labor selection, the "No, Moniek, you stay with me" directive. She remembers him first mentioning the gas chambers.

She began to put the pieces together. As Max revealed some of the dark childhood memories he'd hidden, Frieda remembered some shudder-inducing conversations with her own mother.

Like Max in Warsaw, Frieda had been chased as a young girl on the way home from school in South Dallas. Non-Jewish children had hurled rocks at her and her friends. "Dirty Jews," Frieda remembers them shouting.

"Mom, we're being chased," Frieda had told Rose one day after making it home from school.

Rose told her it would be okay, it would be alright. But she made no active attempt to interfere, Frieda says.

"Fortunately, no one was ever hurt," Frieda says, but the antics left an impression. She didn't tell Max about the rock throwing because she "just thought it was natural" that people throw rocks at Jews.

Frieda also remembered when she first heard rumors about massacres in Poland and Germany.

"Mom, what's all this I hear?" Frieda remembered asking. She was twelve. "What's all this I hear about Jews being killed?"

"*Sha*," Rose replied sternly. "The neighbors will hear." The conversation was over.

"People were frightened that they would come here," Frieda would later say of the Dallas Jewish climate in 1940. "So they kind of stayed within themselves. We were told not to talk about it.

"That was my first inkling of the Holocaust."

Thirteen years later, listening to Max on the Longboat Key drive, she began to understand a little more. She accepted some of the ramifications of his trauma. Frieda grew up in a home that followed the Jewish dietary laws of *kashrut* (kosher food) strictly. Max's family lost the privilege of eating kosher when the Nazis restricted their rights, and now he no longer felt a need to keep kosher. He explained that on the drive, Frieda says.

"He said, 'Frieda, in order to survive, I had to eat anything I could find,'" she remembers. "'It didn't matter if it was kosher or not kosher.'

"Things like that would come out as we're sitting there casually. I don't ever remember in those days asking him a pointed question."

Max doesn't recall opening up on the Florida drive.

"I don't remember what I said yesterday."

<hr />

Max and Frieda would have preferred to stay in Dallas. Max was excited to pursue more education through the G.I. bill. He was ready to enroll in classes to learn how to make and repair upholstery and how to fix televisions; he was hunting for his professional niche.

Their finances dictated otherwise.

"I wasn't going to go through the period of trying to learn while I had to eat," Max says. "So I had to get jobs."

He decided he'd go back to Atlanta to reclaim his pre-draft job at the economy shoe store, Edward's.

But when Max and Frieda arrived in Atlanta, the store owner said he had no openings in Atlanta. He relocated the newlyweds to a store in Gadsden, Alabama. The Jewish community was nice but small in Gadsden, Max says, and some of the non-Jewish locals weren't friendly. Customers slipped religious literature under the store's front door, imploring Max to convert. Some proselytized as they tried on shoes.

Then the Ku Klux Klan began labeling shoeboxes in Max's store. "KKK," the labels read. "Don't buy from a Jew."

It was a far cry from the Jewish shoemaker who had personalized clogs for Max growing up in Warsaw, who had measured each foot by hand and then crafted a custom fit with toothpicks and a hole puncher.

Max tried to peel some KKK labels off and switch out the boxes for other pairs. But he never reported the antisemitism. In a small town like Gadsden, he says, the gesture wasn't uncommon.

"There was always something in the paper that happened," he says. "Somebody did something."

Within less than a year, Max and Frieda rented a trailer, hitched it to their Chevy, and returned to Texas. The Jewish community was stronger in Dallas. Frieda's family eagerly awaited their return.

"Alabama was not for me," Frieda says simply.

Back in Dallas, Max worked first at Walter Hogg Cotton Industries, making cotton for upholstery. He then joined Neiman Marcus to buy and sell ladies' handbags, shoes, and toys, which he continued to do into the 1960s. Max worked for D Play Yards and its expansion store, Southwest Toy and Sporting Goods, before joining his brother-in-law at Imperial Garment Supply Inc. and National Embroidery in the 1970s. Eventually, Max bought Imperial Garment Supply, which he would run until his retirement in 2003.

A love for the toys he had missed in childhood can be traced through Max's professional pursuits. But his main goal was not to do any job for its own sake; it was to support his family. He is proud to say that "I never was unemployed, and I never drew any unemployment checks."

Still, the job he would care about most over the next half-century would prove to be the hardest: being a father.

# CHAPTER 19

# Max the Dad

n the summer of 1954, Max and Frieda were expecting. Max was ecstatic to bring a child into the world. He also felt clueless.

"I was not a baby," Max says of his distorted childhood, "so I didn't know how to be a parent."

The lessons came quickly when Phillip Irwin Glauben arrived on August 25, 1954. When Frieda went into labor, Max parked down the street from Florence Nightingale Maternity Hospital and rushed her inside. But he didn't pay attention to the parking hours, and when he eventually went back to the car after Phil was born, he found that he had received a ticket. He was "so mad," Frieda remembers. He wrote a judge to appeal his ticket: *How did I know it was going to take my wife all this long?* Max won the appeal and didn't have to pay the fine. "I never give up," he says.

Max and Frieda wondered whom to look to for their parenting style. Max didn't think that Warsaw parenting in the 1920s and 1930s was a relevant model. Frieda felt her own parents' style—allowing the kids to do whatever they wanted so long as they didn't ruin the family name— was a bit laissez-faire. So Max and Frieda set to work figuring things out for themselves. They accepted their doctor's orders to stop waking Phil up for his three o'clock bottle: "Leave the poor kid alone and let him get some sleep," the doctor said. They also embraced the mystery of Phil's belly button sticking out. Max and Frieda took a quarter and taped it over the baby's belly button when he was about six months old. Soon, Phil was no longer an outie.

Three years later, on November 3, 1957, Shari Helaine Glauben was born. But Max and Frieda wanted more than two children. They planned to have a third child soon afterward—that is, until Frieda bent over while making their bed and felt a disc in her spine slip. Her lengthy recovery included spinal fusion surgery and six weeks of bed rest. One doctor warned that another pregnancy would be too dangerous for Frieda; a second doctor disagreed and said Frieda could risk it. And on September 2, 1963, Barry Craig Glauben was born.

"You know what? I don't regret the years' difference," Frieda says, referring to the gap between Shari and Barry. "It kept us going so much longer."

Max's comfort with fatherhood evolved as his children grew. But especially early on, he struggled to parent them. He says of those early years that "maybe they didn't get much father-child play" from their workaholic dad. He usually deferred to Frieda in disciplinary decisions and distanced himself when he didn't know how to react. Max judged his parenting skills harshly.

"He'd step back when he felt like he wasn't doing it right as a father," Frieda says. "I disagree because I felt like you do what you do. They're your kids, not just mine. And yet the kids have grown up with a lot of respect for their father."

Max always loved his children—but the thought of loving and losing them scared him. He found it easier to attend their school functions and eat dinner with them than to directly show affection. Some days, Max would give his kids a kiss or tuck them into bed; others, he offered only a simple hello and walked right past them.

"The goodness is there but the closeness, it's embedded in your defense system: Don't do it because you might get hurt," Max says. "They got my full love as much as I could give after what happened to me."

The emotional wrestling affected Phil the most. Shari and Barry remember a childhood with a happier, more nurturing dad. But Phil, who would go on to earn a master's degree in counseling, realized in retrospect that tactile affection from his father had been rare in his childhood.

"Affection came in strange forms," says Phil, adding that he didn't kiss his dad for decades as an adult. "I never felt like he wasn't a loving dad. I felt like I may not have known him real well. There wasn't a lot of self-disclosure."

And there was no discussion, throughout the 1950s, 1960s, and most of the 1970s, that his father had survived the Holocaust.

———— ● ●● ————

That's not to say that teenage Phil wouldn't have answered "yes" if someone had asked him if his dad had lived through the Holocaust. Phil estimates that he learned, somewhat abstractly, when he was five or six years old, that Max was a survivor. But he had "absolutely no idea" what the Holocaust, much less surviving it, meant. His pervasive sentiment—when he thought about it at all—was simply that there was something Dad wasn't talking about. No way was he going to ask.

"We walked on eggshells emotionally in those days," Phil says.

From Max's vantage point: "They realized Frieda had a mom and a dad, and I didn't. But sometimes you just take life for what it is."

Even Max and Frieda spoke sparingly of the war in the 1950s and 1960s. Engaging in long discussions wasn't their style in marriage nor parenting. Each was stubborn on certain matters and preferred privacy at times. Frieda later wondered whether she should have pushed Max more to open up about the Holocaust, but she considered herself "just a little more of a private individual" and didn't want to tell him everything about her past, either. Focusing on the future worked for both of them. Max channeled his energy into long hours at work to support the family; Frieda cooked, cleaned the house, washed the dishes, and sewed clothes for Max and their children. "A typical housewife," she says. "A *motherly* housewife," Max qualifies. Over time, their household became more emotionally and financially stable.

Max enjoyed family dinners when he got off work in time. Frieda often cooked tuna mushroom casseroles in those earlier, cash-strapped days. She thrilled the kids with meals of fried chicken and onion rings in later years, each kid angling to be served first. Frieda made one main dish, take it or leave it. Conversation at the dinner table was "cordial enough," Phil says. As Max recalled, "We weren't asking too many questions," but the family would catch up on each other's activities. How was the latest synagogue program? What did the kids learn in school? Did they win their softball and baseball games? Max would encourage the kids to talk more at the dinner table as the years went by, so long as they didn't talk while eating. And Max always forbade elbows on the table.

At Neiman Marcus, Max was promoted from his job selling women's handbags and shoes to buying toys for the store. He surprised his kids with the latest toy releases, from yo-yos and Slinkys to Etch-a-Sketches and hula hoops. Phil delighted in Marklin electric train sets and an eighteen-hole wooden mini golf course that he'd lay out across the driveway. Shari loved playing with the first Barbie doll in 1959, interchanging Barbie's head with Ken and Midge's when they arrived in 1961 and 1962. She relished riding on a pink rocking elephant when her friends had simple rocking horses.

Frieda was always the chief disciplinarian, but Max became more involved in these years. The kids, it turned out, had inherited their father's mischief gene. No matter that Max had warned Phil and Shari at the gas station not to touch the machine that would squeeze the water out of rags and towels. When inquisitive Phil did so anyway, sticking a finger between the rollers of the machine, his hand was pulled in too. The result: a broken arm.

And never mind that Frieda lectured the kids to steer clear of the wet tar down the street. Shari ruined her white patent shoes—and vividly learned what gasoline smells like—when she toe-tapped on the tar anyway. And when Max chastised Barry and Phil for talking late at night when they should have been asleep, Max would storm down the hallway yelling, "I've had it! I've had it!" Barry, however, often couldn't resist mocking his dad's accent as he stomped off. "Uh oh," Barry would scream each time, "Dad's had it!" Another time, Phil made indirect fun of Max's accent when Max shouted for Shari to "Come up here!" Phil told Shari to report to their father with mop in hand, and then to feign that she had heard him say, "Come mop here!"

There are many pleasant memories from those years. On a picnic at White Rock Lake, Max was washing his car with a bucket borrowed from his mother-in-law. When he bent down to gather more water from the lake, he accidentally let go and the bucket sank. "We laughed over that so much," Frieda says. Max and Frieda would take the kids to drive-in movies with homemade popcorn stuffed into brown grocery bags and citronella to ward off mosquitoes. They rolled the windows down and enjoyed the film. "It just felt normal for the time," Phil says.

It wasn't until he and his siblings were older that they would realize that their family wasn't quite as "normal" as they had thought.

—●●—

Shari thinks she first learned Max was a Holocaust survivor around her senior year of high school. She was in college before her father started opening up publicly about his past, and friends who attended those speeches would tell her they had never known his history. Shari would reply, "Neither did I." If someone had asked her at age twelve whether

her father had survived the Holocaust, she thinks she probably would have said no.

Phil first heard Max speak about the Holocaust at Richland College in Dallas, when Phil was college-aged himself. He was confused: The father who had raised him was sharing war stories Phil had never known? His dad had an entire history he'd never mentioned in two decades of parenting? Max didn't invite questions afterward, and Phil didn't feel comfortable asking. "We didn't grow up with emotional intensity," Phil reckoned, so prying might cross an unstated emotional boundary. Phil wanted to learn more but didn't know where to start.

"This is going to sound weird, but I was very numb about it," Phil says of his first time hearing Max talk about surviving the Holocaust. "I didn't know much about the Holocaust. It felt like a topic I *should* know about, I should study, and I should be informed about. But I never did."

How were Max's kids supposed to know if he didn't talk about it? Max didn't let them in on the secret of his faux driver's license birthday, much less explain that his mom had presumably been gassed at Majdanek or that his dad had been taken from him and killed at Budzyn. The horrors he had lived through didn't seem appropriate to tell his children. Society in general wasn't talking about the Holocaust in the 1960s and 1970s. Survivors weren't yet speaking out or seeking to educate others. Phil and Shari were among the few Jewish kids in their Old East Dallas schools, and they were just coming to terms with what that religious difference meant. To add to that the burden of what their dad had endured because of that difference? That was difficult, and Max felt it was his duty as a father to ensure his kids could experience "what a normal life is." So he never sat them down to tell them his story. He fretted over how his kids would view him if they knew. He decided he would rather leave that chapter of his past where he then thought it belonged—in the past.

"I didn't tell them because I felt number one, I didn't want them to be exposed to the horrible things," Max says. "But furthermore, if you were my child, and I told you about this, every time you look at me, you feel sorry for me. And I wanted a straight parenthood."

"Unless the kids asked him a question," Frieda adds, "he didn't say anything. He didn't want them traumatized."

Eventually, the dialogue began to change.

# TRANSFORMATION

# CHAPTER 20

# Telling the Kids

I t was sometime in the late 1970s. Barry, now in high school, had joined the Jewish youth group, B'nai B'rith Youth Organization (BBYO). It was his turn to plan his chapter's educational program. He approached Frieda.

"Mom," Barry said. "Do you have any ideas?"

Frieda pointed at Max: "He's sitting right over there."

Barry didn't catch on. How would his dad, the gentle but often-reserved and hesitant-to-express-himself toymaker, solve Barry's need to plan a program for the coming Sabbath? Frieda told Barry that Max could tell teens at the program what Judaism and Shabbat were like in the Warsaw Ghetto.

"Your dad is a Holocaust survivor," Frieda said, acknowledging something that had rarely been mentioned in the Glauben house. "He's got an amazing story to tell."

Barry had known through the years that his father was different. He says he knew vaguely that Max had survived something major, that he would wear long-sleeve shirts at summer baseball games. Even on the weekends, Max wore long sleeves.

"I don't want people to see this," Max had once told Barry, hinting at the presence of his tattoo, when his son had questioned the temperature-inappropriate wardrobe choice.

At the time, Barry felt fiercely that whatever had happened in the past, he didn't want to ask anything that might make his dad feel ashamed. Barry had learned over the years that Dad was stern in rare moments of discipline but more often gentle; that he awoke early, 5 a.m. or so, and went to work, and then he came home for dinner. He and Barry would occasionally throw a baseball or kick a soccer ball in the backyard. In that sense, Barry was the first of his children whom Max played with. But neither at family meals nor in backyard activities did Barry pry into what his dad had hidden up his sleeve—literally. Dad didn't want to talk about it, he figured.

"You didn't know if you were opening up a can of worms and [if] mentally it was going to change the way your father or your mother was," Barry says. "You didn't know if it'd help them. Obviously now we know speaking about things is very therapeutic. But at the time?"

So it was years before Barry learned what his father's life entailed before Max had reached Barry's age. But curiosities about his dad's tattoo left him wondering. With Frieda's encouragement, Barry approached Max: "I'm in charge of a BBYO project. How would you like to talk about the Holocaust?"

———— ●•● ————

Frieda says she began to field calls after word spread that Max had agreed to speak to the teens. Parents asked if they could come listen to Max too. How about their teens who weren't in Barry's BBYO chapter?

Frieda lined folding chairs around the den. The crowd would ultimately fill not just those chairs, but also all the standing room through the kitchen and into the dining room. Barry and Frieda remember the attendance differently: one estimates fifteen people attended, the other thinks it was closer to three dozen. But they agree on the significance of Max speaking at the program.

Max told the teens about Shabbat in the Warsaw Ghetto. Discussing the ghetto, he says, was more in vogue at the time than discussing concentration camps. Max had lived through the most famous ghetto uprising in history. But what about before that? How did he practice his Judaism in the confines of the overpopulated, decrepit ghetto?

The teens' questions flowed. Max explained how they commemorated Passover without matzah, and he translated from Polish and Hebrew the blessings he had once recited before meals. Barry, like his siblings when they first heard their dad's story, struggled to internalize that the ghetto challenges—less brutal than some of Max's camp stories—befell *his dad.*

"The first time, it was like 'Wow, he lived through shit,'" Barry says. "When you think about what he had to live through to get to this point, and you're worried about whether you're going to get a new ping-pong paddle or baseball bat?" He pauses. "Inside, it's tearing me apart."

Moments like these also began to tear Max open, or at least prod him to open up. For decades, Max's European and American lives had remained largely those of two different men. He had shielded his kids from the horrors of the war years and avoided sharing the stories with his coworkers. When he had returned to Germany in the late 1950s for a toy fair with Neiman Marcus, Max kept observations about the country's emergence from ruins to himself. He "wanted to be normal," he says, and forced labor and life as an orphan were a far cry from the normalcy he craved.

But as he became more comfortable discussing the war in public, Max began to accept more regular speaking engagements. Friends, family, churches, schools, and others wanted Max to speak as well. Requests multiplied, and he began to give speeches at least weekly, sometimes more often, continuing past age ninety.

"As the years have gone by, he's in demand," Frieda says. "They realize the end of his life is coming. He's ninety years old. How much longer is he going to be able to speak?

"I guess they want to glean as much out of him as they can."

# CHAPTER 21

# Confronting the Past

Max and Frieda trace his path to active Holocaust remembrance and education differently.

At first, Frieda says, Max's post-retirement plan centered around the woodworking skills the Nazis had abused during his pattern-making years. He decided he would make little wooden toys for kids who "have not," Max told her, so "they will all have." Then one day, he walked into the house with a new plan. God had spared his life for a reason, Max decided. He needed to educate. He would devote his time to teaching about the Holocaust.

Max estimates he first delivered a speech on his Holocaust experiences in the mid-1970s. He wasn't sure what to say. Many specific memories were still traumatic.

"I wasn't that well-informed" about the Holocaust in those years, Max says, comparing himself to a prison inmate lying in a cell. The inmate may have intricate knowledge of his cell, but can he really speak knowledgeably about the jail beyond it? How accurate or meaningful would those descriptions be? And how would the inmate convey the pain of life in the jail cell to the listener?

So Max decided he could speak about singing in the camps and his job making patterns for airplanes, about beds stacked three-high in barracks and rations amounting to a single slice of bread with burnt wheat coffee. He couldn't vouch for what went on inside every building in those camps, how prisoners in other camps fared, or what the Nazis had planned with regard to relocation and labor strategy.

"It was all internal I was speaking," Max says of his limited scope.

He set out to learn more. He would reclaim his survivor identity in a series of rapid-fire developments.

Max joined a Dallas-area Holocaust survivors group in 1977 to begin planning for a local memorial. In 1978, the group educated students regionally and began working with the Anti-Defamation League and Nazi war criminal investigations. By 1979, they had successfully launched a campaign for the Dallas Memorial Center for Holocaust Studies, to be housed at the Jewish Community Center. The memorial center was formally established April 15, 1984.

Max also joined the first-ever American gathering of Jewish Holocaust survivors and their descendants in 1983. More than twenty-thousand survivors and their families flocked to Washington, D.C. IBM computers enabled survivors to enter their names into a Holocaust survivor registry through congressional records. Frieda encouraged Max to opt in. Maybe if Max was in the database, he could reconnect with long-lost relatives. It was a possibility he dreamed about, but not one he realistically expected to see happen.

On April 22, 1985, however, that dream came true. Two of Max's aunts, Hanna and Irene, found him through the registry and called. They arranged a reunion in Philadelphia. Max wondered how it would go.

"I knew I was a strong one," he says. "But how would they react?"

Max hadn't seen either aunt since arriving in Majdanek forty-two years earlier. He had long assumed they were selected for death and then sent to the gas chambers. Instead, Max discovered, Hanna and Irene had been assigned to a munitions factory in Leipzig, Germany. Hesitantly—

and with no small amount of hope—Max asked his aunts whether his mother and Heniek had miraculously managed to be selected for labor also. Neither had.

Still, Max was ecstatic to reclaim family members.

"I started yippie-de-do-dahing it," Max told *The Dallas Morning News*, which featured the reunion on the newspaper's April 24, 1985 front page. "It's a one-in-six million shock."

This high-profile reunion, Max says, is "when it all became real." His story's reach "really started multiplying." Max then became president of Dallas' Holocaust survivors advisory board in 1988, and the release of the film *Schindler's List* in 1993 created a further platform.

"Survivors saw the public really was receptive to the Holocaust story," says Rabbi Meir Tannenbaum, a Holocaust educator who worked intimately with Max in Dallas. "They said, 'Wait, why don't you hear my story? I lived that life too and my story didn't end as well as *Schindler's List* did.'"

By 2003, when Max retired from the professional world, the Dallas Holocaust Museum was proposing to relocate to the city's downtown, across from the Sixth Floor Museum that memorializes President John F. Kennedy's assassination. The Holocaust museum had become far more than what its founders had initially envisioned, a place for survivors to commemorate lost family members and the Jewish community to educate themselves on their people's darkest era.

The museum had evolved into a citywide initiative now—a regional educational resource even. It was time to tell everyone about this chapter in history.

But Max worried: How could he be sure he was telling all the details accurately?

# CHAPTER 22

# Going Back

The questions raced through Max's mind: What if sixty years removed, he had started to blur details? What if his memories had blended with stories he had learned in research, or his memory had blotted out stories imperative to capturing his wartime experiences?

"After you tell the truth for a million years, you become doubtful," Max says. "What if somewhere along the line, maybe it wasn't so?

"My number was 14732. I've been telling it for seventy years. But I said, 'Max: What if at one time you made an error and continued with that error?'"

Returning to Poland after so long, he realized, could reassure him about his memories. The opportunity arose in 2005.

Students from Yavneh Academy, a Jewish high school in Dallas, had been visiting concentration camps in Poland as part of an international Holocaust remembrance and education program called March of the Living. The program, named after the death marches like the one Max was forced to make from Flossenbürg, organizes treks throughout Poland in concentration camps and Jewish community sites. Visitors study the perils of prejudice, intolerance, and hatred. And on Holocaust

Remembrance Day every year, thousands from across the globe march 1.3 kilometers from Auschwitz labor camp to Birkenau death camp.

March of the Living organizers strove to pair delegations with Holocaust survivors. In Yavneh's case, the fit was natural. The school invited Max.

And he couldn't wait.

Frieda was less sure of the idea, though.

How would Max react, returning for the first time sixty years after liberation? Would the sites of torture induce flashbacks? Would the loss of family hang heavier? Would the grief he didn't have the chance to process in the camps finally crush him?

"I could visualize him having a heart attack and passing out," Frieda says. "You imagine you went through all these horrors and you're going back, and going to walk through the crematoria?

"He wasn't going unless I went with him."

Max agreed to the compromise, and he and Frieda joined Yavneh's 2005 trip. While there, however, she kept her distance from him, feeling strongly that her husband belonged to the students while in Poland. Even at nights in their hotel room, Max and Frieda talked sparingly, exhausted by the physical and emotional toll of visiting one valley of death after another. Still, Frieda rose early each morning to style her curly hair.

She braced for the possibility that Max would break or need her support. Instead, Max thrived. He taught, learned, and bore witness. He cried just once, on his return to Majdanek, where Fela and Heniek had been gassed.

"You have to disconnect yourself, and you're like a teacher on an educational trip, not a pleasure trip," Max says. "Just educational."

Divorcing himself from his emotions was a skill Max would become increasingly adept at. Sure, the first trip back was bizarre and surreal as he returned to these sites from his past. But his emotions mostly centered around family memories that flooded back. If he really wanted to—and usually he didn't—Max could cry later. He could wrestle with flashbacks while lying awake at night, the nightmares creeping back into his subconscious. March of the Living, he decided resolutely, wasn't the time for him to cry.

It was the time to act as a gateway between past and present for the teens, helping bring to life the horrors that they couldn't even comprehend. It was the time for Max to confirm that his memories, as unbelievable as each seemed, were accurate and not a tale he had contrived. It was the time to enlighten a new generation of witnesses for the future.

"He made sure the heaviness of the trip and its tragedies taught us," says Reid Cohen, who traveled with Max on the 2012 trip, "but didn't crush us."

Max became addicted to this new sense of purpose, he says.

"Max was on a high," Frieda adds. "I guess he felt like he was making a difference."

He would keep going back.

———◆•◆———

Participants who have witnessed the March of the Living alongside Max over fourteen years cite similar experiences with him as one of their guides. Their memories of Max sharing his memories have made an indelible impact on each one of them, it seems. It's difficult to divorce these memories from the mental image of five-foot-two Max in his oversized blue March of the Living windbreaker, adorned with patches indicating each of the years he marched to bear witness. The jacket, like its owner, shows no signs of fraying, and neither completely betray the depth or breadth of where they have traveled. The jacket has kept its color through repeat visits to centuries-old synagogues and cemeteries, mass graves in forests, and boxcars that have seen horrors no one should have ever experienced. The jacket has shielded its owner from wind, rain, and snowstorms on visits to labor camps and death camps. Its hood has encased the twinkling eyes and wrinkled lips that each year share stories with groups of enrapt teenagers.

On March of the Living trips, especially in the earlier years, Max left a distinct impression of not just emotional but also physical strength, outpacing drained teens with the advantage of youth. Even at sixty or seventy years younger, they don't have his adrenaline to will them forward.

Max beams as the teens sing Jewish songs and celebrate in forlorn synagogues, often making sure that he dances in the center of the circles. Teens clap along as he shakes his hips back and forth with pure elation. His joie de vivre reassures March of the Living participants that they too will forge ahead even after unspeakable atrocities.

Max leaves an impression with the students as he cracks jokes from bathroom stalls. He has strolled the aisles of buses leaving the concentration camps innumerable times, personally distributing hard candies to tear-stained teens. He has answered every question he's been asked and helped teens sort through their confusing emotions.

"Max was a barometer of when we could laugh and when we should just reflect in the moment," says Mika Stein, a March of the Living participant in 2013. "He gave us permission to feel joy and the strength to bear witness to the ruins of tragedy with dignity."

Max still hums and sings the same melodies he once timed to the rhythm of boxcar wheels. The Polish and Yiddish lyrics evoke chills. They also shed light on how he survived such trauma—and on how each of his students can grow out of trauma.

"Max's mental preservation strategies during the Holocaust kept his spirits high and feet moving," 2014 participant Jason Epstein says. "He brought light to every experience in his darkest days and continued to do so for me that day at Birkenau."

Vivid images of Max on the March of the Living imprint themselves in students' memories. They remember Max receiving *aliyot*, or honors with a Torah scroll, at synagogues and ruins across Poland. He received such an honor during his first Shabbat back in Warsaw. It felt to him as if he was reclaiming the Warsaw bar mitzvah he had barely celebrated, "like the culmination of something interrupted and taken away so many years ago," 2005 March of the Living participant Benjamin Epstein says.

**Max with granddaughter Sarah on March of the Living, April 19, 2012.** *Photo courtesy of Arthur David Zoller / zollerphoto.com*

Max continues year after year receiving *aliyot*, closing his eyes as he recites blessings over the Torah scroll that he was forbidden from reading during the war years. He carries the scroll on Holocaust Remembrance Day, and in 2012, even did so arm-in-arm with his granddaughter, Sarah. He's rebuilt a life of family and Judaism not completely unlike the one that had been torn from him.

And each time he returns with teens, he creates witnesses.

# CHAPTER 23

# Let's Go Back Together

"**A**nd that's where I saw the first shot fired," Max says, pointing at his old apartment on Moranofska Street from inside the restored Warsaw Ghetto. He details the conditions during the ghetto uprising and tells students how "in those days we didn't drink any water" after their access to it was restricted. In the ghetto square, Max shares his memory of the Nazi guards ordering the Glauben family out of their hideout when the uprising ended and into this very square for searching and deportation to Majdanek.

Max educates students more about deportation from inside a boxcar in Lodz, another Polish Jewish center of mass deportation and murder during the war. More than seventy thousand Jews were rounded up and deported from Lodz to the Chelmno killing center in 1942, a year before Max's deportation. Boxcars were "the loudest place in the world," Max says from inside the dark wooden chamber, so unlike the peaceful tree canopies just barely visible through a hole in one wall. "And the feeling of, 'Why am I in the boxcar?' Being told you did something wrong…if you weren't the one who did it, you have a guilty feeling and that's how we felt."

He explains how he wasn't fed for five days and how rancid the cramped vehicles were.

"Do you have waste?" he says, recalling the stench from bodily fluids and decaying flesh that still lingers in the air. "Yes. You do. It's humid."

At concentration camps too, Max shares personal stories. At the gates of Majdanek, Max explains the unloading of boxcars and how he was selected for labor. He speaks from the elevated stone monument now marking the camp's entrance. "What was amazing was that you went into a horrible place," Max says from the platform, "but there were lights shining and you see the city. We saw lights over there."

Max insists on descending each step of the monument himself—no, he doesn't want a shoulder for support—before leading teens through high winds and storms to Majdanek's guard house, where a rose garden once contrasted sharply with the murderous selections housed there. The fresh grass and blooming dandelions that grow in the selection area today weren't in the camp then, he says. No life could grow from beneath the mud and rocks on which thousands of barefoot prisoners plodded.

Max tells of spending the night on the metal floors of a portable building near the camp entrance, "with [our] face down so we couldn't do anything."

"We thought they were going to finish us off," he continues. "Because when we were selected, they didn't tell you you were going to a concentration camp. You thought maybe they picked you up to shoot you."

A few tears roll down one teen's cheek; a classmate offers a supportive embrace. Others stare into the distance, trying to process the information. Now indoors, away from the storm, creased notebooks emerge as the teens attempt to chronicle the stories Max is sharing.

Max details the shower, shaving, and clothing processes as the group stands inside the Bad und Desinfektion I (bath and disinfection) barrack. Stale air permeates the damp wooden planks. Max tells of his and Isaak's ride to Budzyn, the day he became an orphan, and the scarring moments from roll call after his father's death. He relays the moment that he became a patternmaker.

Max gestures purposefully to teens sitting on the charred wooden floors of barracks in Majdanek; a camp so intact, historians have said it could be up and running in forty-eight hours. As he explains how he convinced Keller to switch him from ditch-digging to woodworking, it's easy for listeners to imagine the teenage Max and uniform-clad foreman conversing in that same barrack, fumbling with wooden slabs and metal springs.

━━●●●━━

Students begin to get accustomed to the barracks. The clumps of human hair, the luggage, the fragments of pottery hoarded by the Nazis still disturb but no longer surprise. It's hard to believe each belonged to a real person at one point, but each did. Students journey through some barracks that have been preserved to resemble their days of operations and others that have been repurposed for museum exhibits. The number of artifacts the barracks contain is staggering: there are thousands of shoes—sandals and boots, red loafers and tan hiking boots—from victims who never walked out of the camp. Max feels a particular connection with the shoes.

In one Majdanek barrack exhibit, Max traces his finger along a map on the wall, describing each camp he once labored at. He shows his route from Majdanek to Budzyn, from Mielec to Flossenbürg. He circles back to the quick detour he took to Plaszow near Auschwitz/Birkenau, noting that he spent one very scary and uncertain day in the salt mines—but just one.

Majdanek was the last stop for Mom and Heniek, he says. Students try to grasp the import of his words and imagine themselves as Max's family, never leaving the very grounds on which they are now standing. As Max adds that he and other prisoners were moved eastward to avoid the approaching Allies, the teens try to wrap their minds around the interplay of personal story and world history, remembering that history is in fact a compilation of personal stories.

Then the group approaches another barrack. Careful observers notice a ladder fastened to one of the barrack's brick walls. The chimney flares through the middle of the roof. A table dominates the entryway. Nazis prepared bodies for crematoria on that table, visitors learn. The table could easily be mistaken for the table traditionally used to tenderly cleanse Jewish corpses for a dignified ritual burial in normal circumstances. But those who keep walking and turn left at the corner see the ovens.

The iron-and-brick contraptions that look ready to bake a cake "efficiently" burned five human bodies every thirty minutes, Max says. He pauses. It was this crematorium—or one of its sister Majdanek oven houses—where Mom and Heniek would have been reduced to ashes after they were gassed.

Max doesn't lose his calm, but at this point, most students do. Nearly everyone is sobbing now. Max recites the Jewish memorial prayer of *Kaddish*, adding a word to honor the memory of "good lives" rather than simply "lives." It's that emphasis on life over death that pierces everyone's hearts.

The eerie prayer echoes in students' ears as they exit the barrack, eyeing the chimney through which smoke from burning flesh escaped. Next are the steps to a massive monument-like dome, this one at the camp's back gate. The mausoleum, constructed in 1947 to house seven tons of Majdanek victims' ashes, is yet another visual that hints at the enormity of the loss. "Let our fate be a warning to you," reads a Polish inscription overlooking the steps. Again, Max emphasizes the individuality of victims rather than just the mass aggregate: they "belong," he says, "to people who were instrumental."

Max stands beside the seven tons of ashes from those who didn't survive as he did, and he tells the students directly: This happened. It happened to me. Believe it. Tell people. See the loss. Think not of the number six million, but of six million individuals; what Einsteins, Elvis Presleys, doctors, musicians, did we lose in this massacre? Whose operas might we otherwise be listening to? Whose medicines would have cured our diseases?

"When I was sobbing before the ashes of those lost at Majdanek," Dalya Romaner, a 2014 March of the Living participant, says, "I was not thinking about their deaths and how sad that is. I was reflecting on how much life is contained in these ashes."

Live life for each of them, Max says.

# CHAPTER 24

# Here's Why

uschwitz and Birkenau evoke new memories too. Max didn't spend time in either during the war. The closest he came was Plaszow, eighty kilometers away. As it turned out, according to Holocaust scholars, when he and his fellow prisoners were on a boxcar headed toward Auschwitz/Birkenau, the camps didn't have space for them.

Still, he tells stories at Auschwitz and Birkenau that shake the students. Some shudder to learn of prisoners whipping other prisoners, of the perverted experiments Dr. Joseph Mengele performed, of commands to carry corpses toward decaying piles. And were there additional horrors Max endured that he isn't talking about? He largely avoids discussing his personal pain because "pain can't be duplicated. So why talk about it?" Teaching is important, however, he says. Simply disturbing teenagers isn't Max's definition of effective Holocaust education. In quieter moments, though, when the group spreads out, Max shudders.

"The psychological just came back to me," he said at Auschwitz in 2017, "the inhumane ways people were hung."

**The deceptive gates of Auschwitz reading *"Arbeit Macht Frei,"* which translates to "Work Will Set You Free."**
*Photo courtesy of Arthur David Zoller / zollerphoto.com*

Hangings were a double whammy, Max says, not only eliminating some Jews, but also scaring others into submission. Torture awaited those who didn't behave.

March of the Living staffers sometimes wonder whether more emotional descriptions would make stories more memorable. But they tend to agree that there's no one single method for finding the right balance between shock value and emotional empathy. Max's factual accounts resonate.

Max's choice of details—when, how, where—shift slightly each trip. So do the itineraries. Max never reads from a script. He speaks from the heart. His mood and thoughts evolve each year as he integrates whatever information he's discovered since his last visit to Poland.

But the exact details of his stories aren't the main reason that Pam Fine, a psychologist who leads the Dallas delegation each year, tells teens that their job on the trip is to spend as much time with Max as possible. It's not about whether his dad was killed on Thursday or Saturday, how many days exactly he rode boxcars between camps, or which days he finagled one slice of bread or two.

"It's the *gestalt* of Max," Fine says, using the German word that describes one's whole being. "The way he remembers things, cares about the kids, and wants to share this with them."

His message of how futile hate is, Fine says, is the key to teaching teens how to move forward. Harboring hate for his tormentors would hurt him more than them, Max came to realize. Instead, he insists on promoting a worldview in which people are essentially good. Max radiates a love of life that's magnetic.

"The greatest thing Max does for the kids is to [help them] realize if there ever is a person who should be angry, it would be him," says Rabbi Meir Tannenbaum, who traveled with Max as Yavneh's March of the Living educational director from 2005 to 2018. "Yet he's not angry because he recognizes the fallacy of anger—that anger is counterproductive."

Teens indeed wonder how Max isn't angry. Why doesn't he hate people from his past? Why doesn't he blame God? Max's faith is his answer. Does he convince everyone who asks these questions? Not necessarily. But "even if they don't understand the God-in-the-Holocaust equation," Tannenbaum says, "knowing that someone like Max has no problem believing in God is very powerful. It forces them to reevaluate the question and say, 'Why is it that Max doesn't ask this question and I am?'"

Max doesn't let an inability to explain why millions were murdered in the Holocaust cloud his faith in God. Believing in free will makes blaming God intellectually dishonest, he says. Max watched humans commit the horrors of the Holocaust. He believes God was with him as he survived. Teens leaving Auschwitz and Majdanek search for God in their lives, too.

"This trip brought up a huge number of questions which remain unanswered," says Sophia Fineberg, a 2018 March of the Living participant. "Max and his sense of spirituality inspire me to keep searching for answers—but also to continue believing even if I don't receive the information I desire."

Max reassures students who struggle to reconcile a higher power with mass murder. He has fostered belief in nonbelievers.

"I've never told anyone this and don't intend to," one participant wrote Max in a letter after a 2010s trip, "but you're the reason I believe in God now."

◀●◆●▶

Faith in God and faith in humanity are among the most powerful messages Max teaches at the camps, more than a dozen March of the Living alumni say. But Max's lessons are many, they add. He teaches them not to hate; to understand, accept, and love others. Move on and look forward, like a soldier in the army who never retreats. Take advantage of the freedom to pursue a formal education. Practice religion freely. The Jewish people are a tribe of strength and resilience, not simply a group of victims.

Rabbis and teachers preach the same messages. They can't preach with the moral authority Max does, Tannenbaum says.

"Someone who lived through the Holocaust yet has no room for anger? Someone who lived through it and preaches against hate? Someone who lives through it and says God was right there? You can't replace it.

"We can tell that to them but it doesn't mean anything compared to when Max says it to them."

# CHAPTER 25

# His Eyes Shine...

Max's impact on March of the Living participants surprises them. Most end up flocking to him by trip's end, treating him like a celebrity while feeling that he cares about each of them deeply and personally. Plenty of them already had noticed Max in the front row of the synagogue in Dallas where they grew up, a wide smile across his wrinkled face making them prouder of the ritual they'd just observed. Max has traveled to Poland enough times now that teens hear from friends, cousins, and siblings what he has done for them. They look forward to—even crave—the chance to learn about the war from Max; from a person rather than a book, and from inside the camps in Poland rather than in classroom chairs in Texas.

"Bridging the gap between 'ancient' history and modern times," Zach Epstein, a 2017 March of the Living participant, says, "allowed me to see the Holocaust as a fairly recent event, and one that is still extremely relevant today."

A camp like Majdanek is "so real and so preserved that it terrifies me," Romaner says. But Max has a way of assuaging that fear, she wrote in a poem on the 2014 trip.

"I look at his face," the poem begins. "The lines tell of a childhood of suffering and horror/ but his eyes show youth."

She continues:

> *His eyes shine with the fulfillment of his life*
> *The lines burst out from the corners of his youthful eyes,*
> *Like rays of sunshine brightening our lives.*
> *His face tells a sad story, but his eyes reveal the story's end.*
> *His face tells of malnutrition and beatings, yet his eyes*
> *show children and grandchildren,*
> *His face teaches history; past, present, and future.*

It's a face that doesn't "look like a survivor," students say. Max's smiling demeanor, utter normalcy, and unimposing stature defy assumptions of a worn survivor. He doesn't *look* like he was starved and beaten and tortured, teens say.

"It was later I realized that being a survivor doesn't come with physical traits (besides the tattoo)," 2009 March of the Living participant Rose Kreditor says. "That the survivors of the Holocaust were people who came from families and communities like ours."

Max is a husband, father, and grandfather, just like their own dads and grandpas, the teens realize. He still called home to Frieda from outside the barracks so she wouldn't worry. He spoke proudly of his latest grandchild earning a degree from Texas A&M, another making the cheer squad at Michigan, a third expecting Max's first great-granddaughter. He still goes to the synagogue, says blessings, and makes sure to celebrate his Judaism with rituals he was forbidden from performing during the Holocaust.

"He highlighted silver linings and made each of us recognize our own fortunes in life," 2010 March of the Living participant Daley Epstein says. "He regularly expressed gratitude for his own and an almost child-like sense of awe regarding the goodness of life's opportunities."

2012 March of the Living participant Ilana Wernick marveled at how the weight of Max's trauma didn't depress him. "Max saw it as an opportunity to build for the future."

The witnesses he inspires see it the same way.

—•••—

Take Bess Reisberg.

Eight years after going on the March and seeing Majdanek through Max's eyes, Reisberg was teaching honors science at Danforth Junior High in Wimberley, Texas, a town thirty-eight miles southwest of Austin and with a population of three thousand.

Danforth's eighth-grade literature curriculum includes a Holocaust unit. Students read *Night* by Elie Wiesel, a survivor of Auschwitz and Buchenwald who won the 1986 Nobel Peace Prize. The students also pore through Anne Frank's *The Diary of a Young Girl* and select Holocaust-related topics while honing their research and citation skills.

But connecting to the material can be challenging. Teachers wondered how best to help students in Wimberley, which identifies as more than 90 percent white, connect with what it's like to be a minority.

A Danforth teacher, knowing the town had a sparse Jewish presence, posed an idea to Reisberg: Would she be willing to speak to the students about her experiences as a Jew?

Reisberg considered the request and decided to expand on the idea. She cobbled together a PowerPoint presentation of pictures from her March of the Living trip, including numerous experiences that Max had shared. She interspersed images of large pits that had been dug in Polish forests to serve as mass graves along with pictures of shoes and personal items that had been confiscated from Jewish prisoners in concentration camps. She organized all of this into a lesson to be delivered strategically.

First, she wanted to consider her students' perspectives. "We've all lost someone we know and gone to cemeteries," she says, but she wanted to emphasize in her talk to the students how in the Holocaust, untold numbers of Jews were incinerated or buried in unmarked graves. The Nazis also ransacked existing Jewish cemeteries, plundering tombstones that could be used for concrete infrastructure in service of the war effort. Reisberg showed students photos of Auschwitz in the present day, when ten thousand March of the Living participants flood the camp on Holocaust Remembrance Day.

And Reisberg didn't shy away from showing heart-piercing crematoria images. As she displayed a picture of the seven tons of ashes in Majdanek, she reminded the students that she took these pictures herself, that she walked these camps herself, that she was presenting to them undeniable evidence the Holocaust occurred.

"It's really hard to believe that people don't even think that this ever happened," said a Danforth student named Tori. "I hope that by learning this, we won't repeat it."

"Still can't wrap my mind around the fact that people had the heart to hurt so many people," wrote another student, Kati.

Reisberg didn't shy away from the more troubling aspects of the narrative, whether she talked about the Holocaust generally or specifically about the trauma Max endured, including the deaths of his mother, father, and brother. "I wasn't sugar coating," Reisberg says. Students "need to be shocked a little bit. Seeing it actually exists [is a] bringing-down-to-earth moment of reality."

Reisberg implored students to learn about their own family history, to explore worlds and cultures beyond Wimberley. Understanding is essential for combating hate, she told them. She left the students with this advice: don't walk away from here scarred by the lows to which humanity can sink; walk away ready to ensure that such cruelty must never go unchecked again.

"In eighth grade, they have all the potential in the world," Reisberg says. For her as a teacher, it comes down to a simple question: "What kind of person do we want to be?"

Echoing Max nearly verbatim, she told each student that they have the potential for both good and evil. They each have to decide: Will I feed my potential for evil or for good? Reisberg couldn't know for sure how many students her message reached, how many thought it preachy. But one student, whom Reisberg describes as a typically angry and distant teen, opened up in a letter following their conversations.

"People have so many different stories to tell," the student wrote. "Stories that build America. Thank you for opening my mind just a little more to really explore what the world is trying to tell me."

Reisberg's takeaway?

"She realized how much more is out there."

Age notwithstanding, Max still creates witnesses directly. He lectures in the United States and Europe, indulging interview requests from newspapers, magazines, and TV stations. In 2014, Max delivered a speech at the United Nations in New York. In 2019, The Dallas Morning News selected him as its Texan of the Year.

Max's witnesses, like Reisberg, compound this effect by incorporating his testimony into their own teaching. In addition, Holocaust scholars and museum professionals seek even more ways to preserve his testimony. One organization that has helped Max record his legacy is the University of Southern California's Shoah Foundation—The Institute for Visual History and Education.

Founded in 1994 by director Steven Spielberg in the wake of his film *Schindler's List*, the institute conducted nearly fifty-five thousand audio-visual testimonies in its first twenty-five years. It also partners with USC's Institute for Creative Technologies to develop and manage digital collection technologies.

Shoah Foundation staffers filmed Max during the 2019 March of the Living as part of a project to one day enable visitors to digitally access a 360-degree tour with survivor testimonies. They also selected Max for a project closer to home. At the Dallas Holocaust and Human Rights Museum, visitors have begun to cherish its impact.

# CHAPTER 26

# Virtually Eternal

## April 25, 2019

A smile animates Max's cheeks as he begins to sing along with a video clip.

*Gliiiick. Izdoch farhannen un ah shir. Nitvamir un nitvadir. Vuzvet desof meiner zein.*

"Luck," he later translates the ghetto-era hymn he didn't write but relates to deeply. "There are different types of luck. Not for me and not for you. What's my end going to be?"

It's a Thursday afternoon at the Dallas Holocaust museum, and Max Glauben is in a lecture room that for years he has visited to deliver near-weekly speeches. He has trekked countless times to his post at the front of the room near a corner lectern, his eight-ounce water bottle and assorted chocolates tucked reliably into its shelf.

But today, Max has settled into a gray chair. Frieda sits in one to his left. Max isn't here to deliver a typical speech. The videoed clips that he will watch today—displayed on an eighty-two-inch screen covering a door by the front right corner of the room—are different. Today, Max and his family are beta-testing the latest technology from the Shoah Foundation's interactive Dimensions in Testimony project.

Max's children and grandchildren take turns holding down a mouse while speaking into a microphone to ask questions of Max's permanent digital testimony. Max is the nineteenth survivor that the Shoah Foundation recorded for an interactive digital testimony. With cutting-edge technologies in natural language processing and volumetric recording, the Shoah Foundation team is creating a program that understands audience questions and prompts Max's responses from a library of pre-recorded options. The Shoah Foundation filmed Max's 1,146-answer collection across five days in August 2018, each response recorded from twenty-three camera angles. Max is amazed that he lived long enough to see such digital advancement.

"It must be a godsend in technology that this is possible," Max says, referring to the projection, "and that there are some of us that have been given a few extra years to be on this earth and deliver our testimony."

Hearing the lyrics translating to "what's my end going to be?," Max is simultaneously transported back to the 1940s, when he first learned and sang this song, and to the future, as he envisions how many Dallas Holocaust museum visitors will one day hear him carry this tune. He knows now, more than he did in the 1940s, what his end will be. The eighty-two-inch projection foreshadows that destiny.

Present-day Max gazes intently at the projection of himself filmed nine months earlier. He alternates between admiring and scrutinizing his performance. A viewer can ask the projection of Max on the screen what the Holocaust was, if his family disappeared, or in which concentration camps he was imprisoned. He will answer all questions.

"The boxcar took my family to Majdanek," the recording of Max says. "I was then taken to Budzyn, Mielec, Wielickza, and the final destination of Flossenbürg as a first transport to Germany." The testimony pauses, Max thinking carefully for a moment before he adds: "of Jews."

Present-day Max's eyes widen at his recall nine months before, the suspense of an extra detail clarifying his memory.

"I thought I forgot!" he tells his grandchildren before rolling his eyes back into his head and sticking out his tongue. Max compares his artificially intelligent self to Amazon's Alexa, whom he calls a "little lady in a box."

For nearly two hours, the afternoon proceeds similarly. Max wavers between mouthing words along with his projection, praising his eloquence, correcting his memory ("I forgot May is after April, not before!"), and criticizing his posture. ("Put your hand down!") He's proud that he needed just four and a half minutes when asked to summarize his testimony in five. He's quiet as he watches himself recount some of his worst memories from the ghetto, including when a guard killed a nursing woman and her baby. The same recording mentions another mother, baby in arms, who had gone "berserk" from the decrepit ghetto conditions. "God," she said. "Why is this happening?" Max's recorded response explains that he never believed God was the cause of these horrors; human perpetrators and bystanders were.

It would be easy to confuse the live Max for the recording. At the beta test, he sports a blue-and-white floral button-down shirt, similar to the solid, light blue button-down he wore the day the testimony was filmed. Neither in baldness nor in wrinkles has he visibly aged since the day of the filming. His beliefs and his memories are consistent.

Still, Max "was fearful" on his way to the museum to test the beta technology. He wondered: Would he be educated enough to understand beta testing? Would his testimony be clear and intelligible? But with each question his granddaughter Delaney asked into the microphone, Max became more calm.

"Amazing how I answer the questions so people can understand it and become relaxed," he says. "I think it's fabulous this guy knows what he's talking about."

Max considers: What question does he want to ask himself? It's a strange opportunity and different feeling, he says, than merely watching a recorded speech he's delivered. Because here "I see myself talking to an audience of which I am a part of," Max says. "It's reality." He repeats that he believes testimony opportunities like this are why his life was spared. Just as the Hebrew Bible commands farmers to leave a corner of each harvest crop for the poor and needy, Max imagines his survival similarly: he is among the survivors left in the corner from which the world will partake. It's imperative that he give over his story.

The interactive testimony creates witnesses. It also conveys how Max connects with his audiences through jokes, gestures, facial expressions, and comments in present day formats.

"He's got this warmth to him," says Kia Hays, a project manager for Shoah Foundation collections. "He has a little bit of a twinkle in his eye when he's speaking, and he's very open and he really tries hard to bring you in to what it is he's trying to share with you."

**Max and Frieda (second from left) with children Phil (left), Shari and Barry on September 17, 2019.** *Photo courtesy of the Glauben family*

Recorded clips of Max can tell visitors his favorite sports team (the Dallas Cowboys); how he met his wife, Frieda; and what his favorite food is. But he can be indecisive on the projection as he is in real life; when Delaney asks him his favorite food, the projection queues up a clip of Max's answer: gizzards.

Another time he's asked this same question, a different clip plays: "I don't want to say it," he replies this time, "but...STEW!" He booms the final word. Another time, Max-on-screen says his favorite food is fried chicken.

"You don't like fried chicken," Frieda says to Max, both present and projected. "It depends on the day," real-life Max tells her, grinning at each mention of his favorite foods.

The Shoah Foundation is intent not to emphasize the bizarre if not amusing scene of two Maxes in one room. Two-and-a-half million dollars in funding were donated to ensure the preservation of Max's testimony for generations of Dallas Holocaust and Human Rights Museum visitors. With its September 2019 launch, a computer beams up a projection of Max into a three-dimensional theater space. The system's fully three-dimensional hologram technology remains in the research and development stages. But the Foundation recorded Max with multiple cameras from twenty-three angles to eventually merge his testimony with the three-dimensional technology. In addition, the system's language recognition capabilities grow smarter each time the program is asked a question. In beta testing, for example, museum visitors asked whether Max had experienced antisemitism and prejudice after the war. In response, the system queued up Max's memory of the KKK tarnishing his shoeboxes in 1954.

"He's talking about discrimination not only still being present, but he experienced it in his adopted country—which is our country," Hays says. "That's something really powerful [to make] us realize it's not just part of history. That intolerance is something that's just everywhere and still exists. We constantly have to be educating ourselves against it."

Museum visitors came to ask about the particulars of Max's life stages from Warsaw to Dallas. What did he eat in the ghetto? What did the ghetto smell like? Was Max ever able to have fun in the ghetto? They wondered whether Max hates the Germans, whether his nightmares persist, and what gave him hope to survive.

The testimony divulges both history and philosophy. Max muses about how many new witnesses the recordings will reach.

"Any child, any grandchild, any parent, any grandparent," he says, "could come and listen to us survivors way after we are gone."

# Life as Max Glauben's Grandchild

ax's grandchildren are among those witnesses who have learned directly from him. That astonishes him too. Max remembers vividly when he became a grandfather on June 24, 1985. He had reconnected with his aunts two months earlier and now had proof that not just one but at least two generations of Glaubens could carry on the family name he had fought to preserve.

"That was an unbelievable feeling," he says, "because I never thought I'd live long enough to have married kids—much less grandkids." It was a stage in life his own parents and brother never reached.

Max has seven grandchildren: Sarah Nicole, Ross Isaac, Hayley Megan, Alec Drew, Blake Ian, Delaney Rose, and Madison Brianna. (American names have been known to confuse Max, who speaks with a distinct accent heavily influenced by his six languages. "Medicine?" he asked, puzzled when he heard the name Shari had given his seventh grandchild. "Like a prescription? Why would you name her that?") And he has embraced life as a grandfather more easily than he embraced life as a father. For one thing, he says grandparenting is "less responsibility" but also "the joy of life." He refers lightheartedly to a needlepoint Frieda once made that carries the old saw, "If I knew how good it was to have grandkids, I'd have had them first." Max had more clearly reconciled his Holocaust and American experiences by the time he became a grandparent. The grandkids felt more comfortable asking their "Zayde" questions than their own parents had. Max was also more comfortable answering, though he was careful what and how he told them about the Holocaust.

**Max's grandchildren in 2016**
**L to R, back row: Sarah, Hayley, Delaney, and Madison;**
**L to R, front row: Sarah's husband Brett, Ross, Blake, and Alec.**
*Photo courtesy of the Glauben family*

Sarah remembers sitting on Zayde's lap at age four or five, reading books and discussing profound questions in child-appropriate terms:

What does it mean to have people in your country who don't like you and are making rules against you?

Hayley thinks she was middle school aged when she told her friends she wanted the letters "KL" tattooed onto her arm like Zayde had. She figured the ink would remind her and others what her grandfather had survived. She told Max. He was stern.

"This was one of the worst ways the Jews were defaced," Max told Hayley. "And I do not want you defaced like this."

By high school, Hayley was seeking out library books to quench her desire to better understand the Holocaust. She was taken aback the day she read one and realized: *If the Allied soldiers hadn't come that day, I could literally not be living right now.* Max implored her not to become angry or resentful. Share our story instead, he told her, and take solace. Because "I do have a Zayde," Hayley says, "and he's still here."

Each grandchild learned about the Holocaust differently, but their experiences as Max's grandchild comprise more lessons about life than lessons about death. Max's grandchildren learned from him patience in the car, because if Zayde's driving, he's driving slowly and listening to music from the 1920s or 1930s. Trying to change the radio station, says Sarah, "did not end well for anybody." They also learned not to act out before dinner because "Glaubens don't do 'hangry' well," Ross says. They learned that their parents and grandparents could be passive-aggressive but would mostly smile and chuckle their way through life. Max's grandchildren learned to be wary when friends come over: Glaubens are liable to tell dirty jokes. Max generally erupts in laughter before a joke's ending, dirty or clean, because he remembers how much he loves the punchline. Sometimes, when he gets to the punchline, it doesn't make sense. His grandkids learned to laugh anyway. And when their parents were away, Max was known to teach them a Yiddish cuss word or two.

When the grandkids would sleep over at Max and Frieda's, they would ask: Why does Zayde wake up before the sun, around five o'clock?

Was it because he was conditioned to his American professional schedule, or routines during the war in Europe? Does he sleep restlessly after living a constant nightmare through his childhood and teen years? What are his nightmares like?

Sarah has asked Max: "What's the stuff nobody knows? What are you sitting on?"

The gory details he shared of his ghetto years, before he was even deported, "would have been traumatic enough for an eleven-year-old to have their life screwed up forever," she says. "And that was only the start of his journey."

Max's grandkids wonder when the horrors were at their worst, and what torture and pain Max hasn't told them—or anyone—about. If he doesn't tell them, they fear, nobody will ever know.

That's fine by Max. "Look," he responds gently. "I have a responsibility to make sure what I'm sharing doesn't motivate people to hate more and give them ideas. I have to question what the value is and for what purpose it is" to speak of the worst of the worst he has seen.

Sarah accepts that "he's filtered it out forever." He'd rather teach them to forgive, like he once forgave eight-year-old Blake after Blake begged Zayde to step into the batter's box while he pitched.

"All I remember was throwing a curve ball and wishing I'd never let go," Blake says. "Next thing I knew, Zayde had the world 'Rawlings,' along with some baseball laces, across his thigh. Needless to say, he never faced me again." But Max did forgive.

Max has spoken to a school or synagogue group for each of his grandchildren. Five of them, as well as sons Phil and Barry, have joined him on March of the Living trips.

Walking beside Max out of the death camps he survived imbued them with a new level of pride, they say. Still, they struggled—as did their cousins who didn't go on the March—to reconcile the tragedy that befell their family with their joyous grandfather.

In 2012 at Majdanek, the Glaubens' survival was there for all to see. Max, Phil, and Sarah each flanked a gas chamber wall, listening to Rabbi Tannenbaum speak and then recite the mourner's *Kaddish*.

Sarah wondered how Zayde could bear the pain of returning to where his mom and brother were murdered. And then do it again, every year? She bawled. So did Phil. Max remained outwardly detached.

Then the students on the trip trickled out of the barrack and the Glauben trio had their moment. They didn't say a word aloud, but the hug—"one of the strongest, firmest," Sarah says—spoke volumes.

Max had struggled to reconcile the past, Sarah realized, so she didn't have to. "It's time to think about the future, time to focus on making sure this education and experience continue to happen. It really shifted what I felt like my responsibility was, and role in history."

To be one of Max's grandchildren, the seven believe, means they carry the responsibility to tell his story and combat prejudice, to live with the "outlook of the brighter side of life," Alec says, and "to stand for what I believe is right." The Glauben grandchildren dwell less on the tragedy than they do on the imperative to shape the future, to persevere through their personal challenges, and "to repopulate the world for all that was lost during the Holocaust," Delaney says.

They think twice when a project or exam poses a challenge, realizing that maybe, just maybe, the barrier they are facing isn't insurmountable if their grandfather could survive death camps. They celebrate milestones with zest, dancing heartily at family celebrations, knowing they're at risk of Zayde stealing the show with his own moves. Because, as Ross says, even as Max ages, "he's pretty limber."

There are times when the Glaubens' dark family history weighs on the grandchildren. But when they cross Max and Frieda's doorstep, there is always the candy jar brimming with sweets and the fridge stocked with surprises. There are often cookies. Maybe everything will be okay. And there's always laughter, at times because Max and his six languages get lost in translation. The kids all know to buy groceries at Tom Thumb when instructed to go to "Tom Trum." And everyone in the family knows that after one and two comes "tree."

It's all part of the pursuit to "balance the hero with the man," Sarah says. "We play in that world all the time."

But then there are moments like at the Texas A&M stadium in 2016, when Delaney saw Zayde take the podium on the university's football field before thousands of spectators, including actors, singers, and religious leaders, to preach love instead of hate and urge individuals to be an upstander rather than a bystander. When that kind of moment happens, it's easy to understand why Zayde feels to her like "literally a superstar." While white nationalist leader Richard Spencer was telling an audience across campus at the same time that "America, at the end of the day, belongs to white men," Max was preaching unity and tolerance for all.

"I have never been so proud," Delaney says, of "his desire to make the world a better place."

Max's grandchildren see the lessons that he imparts, his imperative to do rather than to stand by, the timelessness of what he says and who he is. Max doesn't just aim to teach them what was and now is, but also what will and should be.

"He's committed," Sarah says, "to being an inspiration and motivation. Not just a commemoration."

# When My Time Comes to Go

E ven in his nineties, Max still has questions. He accepts he won't find all the answers. So he crafts his own.

Max believes every human being has a purpose on Earth. His mom, dad, and brother must have served theirs more quickly than anyone anticipated. Spending his life hating the Nazis and their enablers is not worth it. "The hater is the one who gets the short end of the stick," Max says, while the "'hatee' does not even know what is happening." Devoting time or energy to blaming the Nazis would mean giving them a second win. Max prefers defiance. He doesn't let Holocaust deniers hurt him, insisting that he's glad he lives in a country with freedoms that include the freedom of speech. "I'm glad they're able to express their opinions," he adds, "so the public at large should see how dumb and stupid and uneducated they are." He reasons through the moral Catch-22s he faced during the war with a similarly frank tone.

"If they asked you what Max did," he says, "I'd say he's someone who stole, lied, cheated, but didn't kill. And he did it to maintain life. It's a true story, even though it's horrible. At least I'm honest about it."

Honesty also demands confronting whatever trauma still lingers. Max doesn't want pity, so he speaks sparingly of the challenges he confronts daily. But physically, like many Holocaust survivors, Max's appetite and digestion never recovered from wartime abuse. He lacked the proper nutrients during those years; and in the camps, he could go to the bathroom only when officers mandated. He never regained bowel regularity. He sustained a bleeding ulcer in the 1960s, after which doctors ordered half of his stomach removed. He contracted Hepatitis C in 1995. In 1996, doctors ordered a full gastrectomy. Max can't be sure what ailments resulted directly from the starvation and wartime conditions he was subject to. But he knows he was physically compromised at liberation. He never fully recovered.

Emotionally, Max's ability to love and trust were permanently tainted. When a house guest, thinking Max isn't looking, grabs a handful of chocolates from the candy jar, Max questions his or her honesty. Max and Frieda aren't short on chocolate. But memories of fellow inmates stealing bread from underneath Max's pillow carry over. He watched as a Polish government, once friendly to Jews, embraced antisemitism; and as friends and neighbors stood idly by while the Nazis worked to exterminate an entire people. Institutions and individuals alike let him down. Add all this to the sense that in America he is different and that others can't relate to his psyche, and it's understandable that Max has made few close friends across more than seven decades in America. Fellow survivors Al Zomper and Jack Pollack, whom he met in the 1940s, felt like brothers. But most other friends he viewed merely as acquaintances. Max couldn't help but wonder who wanted what from him. Were their agendas pure? Small talk and casual conversation never came naturally to him.

"I never developed discussion," Max says. "I never found an outlet."

Family relationships pose the toughest challenge: the aversion to conversation plus the risk of loving again. Max notices other fathers talking and playing with their kids in ways that "because all the things I had in me, I could not face myself to do." He struggles to talk on the phone or even sit down for long conversation with Frieda. He will answer questions but warns he won't lead the conversation. The war hardened him, even as subsequent years of love and laughter chipped away at that shell.

"That's what I missed—to have liaison with the kids," Max says. "With anybody."

And Max wonders: What could he have achieved, discovered, or solved with a full formal education? Could he have created a machine to help humankind or discovered the cure for a terrible disease? Max doesn't think he reached his intellectual potential. That bothers him.

"I don't know whether I'm really the person that could've contributed much more in this world than I am contributing because [I had] less of education and also the unknown," Max says.

Then he remembers he's stronger because he emerged from the war and proud of what he's accomplished in spite of the educational opportunities snatched from him. And Max admits that he's proud of his most profound and creative thoughts with regard to all he has seen. While the Holocaust shaped the impact he's made on the world, it's his insistence on love, tolerance, and positive thinking that make him such an effective educator and speaker.

Southern Methodist University recognized those gifts in 2020 when awarding Max an honorary doctorate of humane letters. He is the "embodiment of human hope, resilience and optimism," the university said.

Max's mission to dismantle hatred is a unique life goal, says Rabbi Tannenbaum.

"This is a person who literally—that's what he wants. He wants the world to be a better place, he wants there to be no anger and hatred," Tannenbaum says. "How many people can say that's their goal in life, to make the world a better place by having no one else be angry and hateful? There are very few people who I know who have that as their mission—that's all they want to be successful."

Max understands he was lucky to survive, says Mary Pat Higgins, President and CEO of the Dallas Holocaust and Human Rights Museum. But he also knows that his luck, far from undermining his tale, serves as evidence that his audience should also cling to hope.

"You don't have to be a superintellect, you don't have to be a super-athlete, you don't have to be incredible," says Sara Abosch-Jacobson, the museum's chief education, programs, and exhibitions officer. "You just have to allow the humanity inside yourself to win out. And he's done that."

Max is still vulnerable though, as he was reminded after a damaging June 2019 storm. Max and Frieda lost electricity, air conditioning, and landline phone connection as storms swept the Dallas-Fort Worth area, winds reaching close to seventy miles per hour, uprooting trees and toppling power lines. Max and Frieda were forced to relocate to a hotel for three days. Max knew logically that he could replace the spoiled food, return soon to the comforts of his own home, and communicate by cell phone. Emotionally, that didn't prevent the storm from resurfacing unsettling memories.

"When the darkness appeared, then I had the flashback of having a home and becoming homeless," Max says. "You get the homeless feeling like you had in the camps or in the ghetto, or some of these things flash back even though this is not as bad."

Psychologically, Max is still scarred by the torture he witnessed and endured. He compartmentalizes emotions while speaking, training himself to numb them as if he's an actor or teacher delivering a story that's not as personal as it actually is. But in the quiet of night, controlling his emotions is more challenging. Max is still chased in his nightmares, unable to outrun his pursuers, just as he couldn't outrun the Nazis during the war. Return visits to the camps trigger more frequent night terrors.

Frieda sometimes awakes to Max screaming in his sleep. "Don't ask me what the heck you're saying," she tells him. There are times when he answers himself after crying aloud. "Not a lot, but he does."

Sometimes, Isaak or Fela or Heniek appear to Max in visions—lost, but never forgotten. He may see their faces in new friends. A local rabbi's physique reminds Max of Isaak; a museum staffer's eyes recall Aunt Selah's. Without accounts that confirm the time and place of Heniek's death, Max still wonders if his younger brother will show up some day. He derives strength from the Jewish imperative to actively mourn loved ones for eleven months, then refocus on moving forward. And Max found an unexpected source of closure in 2019 when his community gathered to bury ashes from Majdanek in the Jewish section of a Dallas cemetery. The burial coincided with the *yahrzeit*, or anniversary of death, on which Max commemorates his parents and Heniek. Seeing ashes from Majdanek buried just five miles from his home comforted Max. For the first time in seventy-six years, he could memorialize his family graveside, as others do.

"I have a place where on *yahrzeit*, it's designated, I can go there and lay some flowers and maybe tell them that I love them," Max says. "Thank them for flying on top of me."

Max imagines his family members' souls floating around him and watching over him. Other times, Max says, it's God—whom he refers to by the Hebrew word *Hashem* ("the name")—appearing amid bright shining lights.

When He appears, Max is ready with a message.

"I believe I have lived a rough life and a good life," Max begins. "I am a believer, and I believe that many of the departed souls have guided me, including God and my relatives. I did good things without profiting by them, and contributed much to the welfare of many students for education.

"I hope that when my time comes to go, *Hashem* will have noticed what I was doing and will allow me to continue my work from His head-quarters to the people downstairs, people such as my family, and to the public at large."

# AUTHOR'S NOTE

I was seventeen years old when I first visited Majdanek, Auschwitz, Birkenau, and Warsaw with Max.

The March of the Living program elicited far more questions than answers.

The history we bore witness to engulfed us.

I struggled to understand how the Holocaust unfolded and how Max—standing, at eighty-four years young, before me—survived it. I reverted to a habit, a coping mechanism that would enable me to table most emotional processing until later: I penned what Max was saying, verbatim.

The salient message had been conveyed before the trip: Our children will not have the opportunity to visit these sites with a survivor. We must learn everything we can from Max. Easier said than done.

The enormity of the Nazi genocide numbed me as I sat on the musty, wooden-planked floors of a Majdanek barrack on April 22, 2012. "I'm not sure I've ever told anyone that before," Max said after sharing one recollection.

Immediately, my responsibility as a witness crystallized.

The remainder of that afternoon, I walked in lockstep with Max along the barbed-wire fence of Majdanek. He reflected on the injustice that led to his family's deportation.

"What are laws made for?" Max wondered aloud as we walked. "To protect us, to punish us for doing wrong? The Germans did everything the other way around."

His tone wasn't bitter. He was matter of fact. Max's imperative to live life to the fullest elicited more sternness than did his reprimands of Nazi torture. I wondered: How, and why, did Max feel that way?

———•••———

I graduated from the University of Texas at Austin and moved back to Dallas in June 2016. The next day, Max and I reconnected at our synagogue. Max had recently received a fresh batch of wartime records from Europe. He was particularly excited about a surviving archive from his father's newspaper. I told Max I was interested in reviewing the records. Perhaps, I suggested before my brain caught up with my mouth, we could combine these documents and his memories into a comprehensive narrative.

That was June.

July elapsed.

Max and I bumped into each other again, this time along the indoor track of our community fitness center. We fell in lockstep, just as we'd plodded together four years earlier in Majdanek. At eighty-eight, Max's gait and wandering mind were still forces with which to keep pace. Max said his colleague had reiterated that week that Max's testimony merited a book.

"I thought I was writing your book," I replied, still largely in jest.

Max didn't miss a beat. He beamed: "That's what I told him."

I stopped mid-step.

———•••———

August 12, 2016, we first set up base camp at Max and Frieda's dining room table. We outlined tentative goals.

Max wanted his memoir to teach readers to respect everyone around them and maintain belief in the good of humanity. He wanted to ensure retelling his history would not create further hate. Max hoped also that any written testimony would paint pictures as vivid as the imagery his oral lectures deliver. He wanted to emphasize that his history is real and recent. We set to work.

A deep dive into Max's oral histories unfolded, beginning with a series of January 1990 interviews with University of North Texas historian Keith Rosen. Documents from Max's camp transfers, displaced-person arrangements, immigration attempts and social workers enriched our narrative and prompted further questions to unleash Max's memories. So, too, did a spring 2017 March of the Living trip when I joined Max again in Warsaw, Majdanek, Auschwitz, and Birkenau. Crucial recollections, including emotions he has trained himself to dissociate from the memories he lectures on, flooded back.

Dallas Holocaust and Human Rights Museum staff members recommended profound resources from Max's archives as well as the broader Holocaust scholarship genre. The United States Holocaust Memorial Museum and Shoah Foundation further augmented our research. Students spanning thirteen years of March of the Living trips illustrated the breadth and depth of Max's impact as an educator. We were intent on corroborating historical context across sources. We took no liberties with the truth.

Max's wife, Frieda, children, and grandchildren generously contributed raw emotion and insight into a Holocaust survivor's family. Frieda's seemingly endless refills of tuna salad and homemade cookies shepherded us through long interviews. Sharing pizza dinners and multicolor birthday cake with the Glauben family revealed further what present-day life looks like for a nonagenarian Holocaust survivor. Thanks, Frieda, for answering my late-night phone calls, even when they interrupted you and Max watching the nightly news.

And of course, Max himself has given me a gift I feel wholly unable to articulate. But let's try.

Max was patient when weeks passed between some of our meetings, and his optimism far exceeded my own for where this memoir would take us. Each time I stressed over the tasks that lay ahead, he reminded me gently of the ground we'd already covered. "We've baked the cake," Max would say. "Anything more will be icing on top." He made me laugh often. He was kind, telling me that he could "hear" whether I was smiling or not from the other side of a phone call. He rarely hung up until he felt sure I was smiling.

**Jori and Max on February 19, 2020.** *Photo courtesy of Jori Epstein*

Max trusted me first with his documents, each of which I'm relieved I never spilled on or somehow ruined. Some documents were intensely personal, including E. Liebowitz's assessment of Max in December 1947, when he was depressed and anxious in the days after he immigrated to America. Max never balked as I poked and prodded for more vivid details and emotions. He rarely tired of my incessant questioning, instead calling me after I left his home to add just one more detail to the already rich narratives he'd unearthed. Some memories Max preferred not to discuss at first. Then he'd advance to whispering them in his raspy voice across the dining room table, as if he were nervous but curious about the consequences of saying them aloud. I'll never forget when Max changed his mind and decided he was willing for his memoir to acknowledge the likely sexual assault he suffered in Flossenbürg. Max was resolute that day: Like countless other painful memories and admissions, perhaps his honesty can help others. Perhaps he can help you.

———◆●◆———

The Holocaust is no more comprehensible to me today than it was in the Majdanek barrack on April 22, 2012. But I am committed—and we hope you, our reader, are too—to the continual pursuit of reckoning with humanity's capacity for hatred and violence.

We must continue to confront history like that of Max's life to better understand the depth to which humanity can sink and, in concert, the immense potential each of us has to stand up for what's right. We seek not simply to remember the Holocaust, but to inspire tolerance education and action.

We want this memoir to serve as an educational resource for middle school, high school, and university-level students. We hope adults will find it digestible, yet poignant. We constructed this memoir with the charm and humor Max infuses in his life's work, aiming to create a framework for you to process and house Max's memories and messages. Max's reflections underscore that heroism emerges not when we hold ourselves to superhuman standards, but rather when we let our humanity prevail.

———◆●◆———

After reading this memoir, you now command the power to perpetuate Max's lessons, to combat prejudice, and to deepen the love and shared understanding between and among diverse communities around you. Never has the need for this been greater.

"If you have any hatred, bigotry, or antisemitism," Max implores, "I hope that after you read this book, you might change your mind."

Now, you are a witness and an upstander.

# ACKNOWLEDGMENTS

Thank you to Max, Frieda, Phil, Shari, and Barry for the time and trust to recount your family's powerful testimony. Thank you to Sarah, Ross, Hayley, Alec, Blake, Delaney, and Madison for deepening our generation's understanding of the responsibility we bear. Thank you to the March of the Living alumni who granted interviews for this narrative: Reid Cohen, Benjamin Epstein, Daley Epstein, Jason Epstein, Zach Epstein, Sophia Fineberg, Rose Kreditor, Jonathan Nurko, Bess Reisberg, Dalya Romaner, Rachel Siegel, Mika Stein, Ilana Wernick, and Maxwell Zucker.

This memoir reflects the generous time, expertise, and mentorship from so many: Michael Berenbaum, Glenn Frankel, Brendan Miniter, Mary Pat Higgins, Sara Abosch Jacobson, Charlotte Decoster, and Kia Hays ensured Max's testimony was chronicled conscientiously.

Pam Fine and Rabbi Meir Tannenbaum's deep understanding of Max and the Holocaust elevated my personal exploration of each. Yavneh Academy's commitment to this mission has impacted the lives of hundreds of Dallas community students over the last two decades.

At the University of Texas, Dr. Carol Mackay scrapped my final compare-contrast essay in her course, instead directing me to type and analyze the two journals I kept on March of the Living. Dr. David Crew's "Remembering the Holocaust" course taught me to distinguish between history and how we remember history. Drs. Stephen Sonnenberg and Thomas Palaima's "Myths of War and Violence" seminar underscored the indelible emotional trauma that war and violence imprint on our souls, and the human considerations we must acknowledge to honestly assess our belief systems.

Dena Weaver, Mike Farris, Kevin Robbins, Paul Begala, David Patterson, Liz Liener, Amanda Herman, Robin Davis Miller, and Mike Dubner guided aspects of this memoir's journey from early research to complete manuscript. Eric Schramm's meticulous edit readied the work to be shopped to publishers. Erica Halpern's creative mind conceived the book jacket design. My editors and colleagues at *USA Today* have consistently embraced and encouraged my pursuit of this project, including NFL columnist Jarrett Bell connecting us with Post Hill Press. Post Hill's Debby Englander, Heather King, and Allie Woodlee masterfully navigated the manuscript to publication.

My parents and siblings have dabbled in editing and proofreading, consulting, and distracting. They're the best support system and comedic relief I could ask for. This book doesn't happen without them.

I'm deeply grateful to each of you.